Linguistics Coordinator

Ling Coord

H – few pages
in file

401.9
B48
1987

Semantic Constraints on Relevance

For my parents
Pauline and Leslie Blakemore

Semantic Constraints on Relevance

DIANE BLAKEMORE

Basil Blackwell

Copyright © Diane Blakemore 1987

First published 1987

Basil Blackwell Ltd
108 Cowley Road, Oxford, OX4 1JF, UK

Basil Blackwell Inc.
432 Park Avenue South, Suite 1503
New York, NY 10016, USA

All rights reserved. Except for the quotation of short passages for the purposes of criticism and review, no part of this publication may be reproduced, stored in a retrieval system, or transmitted, in any form or by any means, electronic, mechanical, photocopying, recording or otherwise, without the prior permission of the publisher.

Except in the United States of America, this book is sold subject to condition that it shall not, by way of trade or otherwise, be lent, re-sold, hired out, or otherwise circulated without the publisher's prior consent in any form of binding or cover than that in which it is published and without a similar condition including this condition being imposed on the subsequent purchaser.

British Library Cataloguing in Publication Data

Blakemore, Diane
   Semantic constraints on relevance.
   1. Semantics
   I. Title
   412   P325

ISBN 0-631-15644-5

Library of Congress Cataloging in Publication Data

Blakemore, Diane.
   Semantic constraints on relevance.

   Bibliography: p.
   Includes index.
   1. Semantics. 2. Pragmatics. 3. Relevance
(Philosophy) 4. Cohesion (Linguistics) I. Title.
P325.B48   1987   401′.9   87-11761

ISBN 0-631-15644-5

Typeset in 11 on 12½ pt Times
by DMB Typesetting (Oxford)
Printed in Great Britain by Billings & Son Ltd., Worcester

Contents

Acknowledgements		vii

1 The Domain of Pragmatics

1.1	The Semantics–Pragmatics Distinction	1
1.2	Indexical Semantics	6
1.3	Linguistic and Non-Linguistic Knowledge	11
1.4	Pragmatics and the Competence–Performance Distinction	18
1.5	Grice's Theory of Conversation	21
1.6	The Problem of Context Selection: Mutual Knowledge Frameworks	27

2 Relevance and Communication

2.1	Grice's 'Calculability' Requirement	34
2.2	Deduction in a Theory of Utterance Interpretation	39
2.3	Deduction and Contextual Modification	47
2.4	The Principle of Relevance	54
2.5	Implicature	63

3 Linguistic Form and Pragmatic Interpretation

3.1	Conventional Implicature	72
3.2	Premises and Conclusions: Evidence and Justification	78
3.3	Premises and Conclusions: Implication and Explanation	85
3.4	Additional Premises	91
3.5	Interaction with Focus: 'also'	97

	4 Relevance and Coherence: Discourse Connectives	
4.1	Coherence in Discourse	105
4.2	Coherence and Content: the Interpretation of Conjoined Utterances	111
4.3	Coherence and Relevance: Inferential Connections	118
4.4	*But*: Denial and Conjunction	125
4.5	*But*: Contrast and Conjunction	131
4.6	Concluding Remarks	141

Notes	145
References	149
Index	154

Acknowledgements

This book, which originated as my doctoral dissertation, owes its existence to the guidance, support, and patience of a number of people on both sides of the world. First, I would like to thank my Philosophy teachers in New Zealand, John Bigelow and Max Cresswell (both then of Victoria University Wellington), not only for their excellent teaching, but also for arousing my interest in language and encouraging me to develop it by going to study Linguistics at University College London.

During the preparation of my dissertation many people listened to and discussed my half-worked-out ideas. I would particularly like to thank Regina Blass, Mike Brockway, Robyn Carston, Annabel Cormack, Ruth Kempson, Stephen Levinson, Neil Smith, and Andrew Spencer. Special thanks are due to Ruth Kempson and Neil Smith for encouraging me to make my ideas more public.

As the reader will soon see, the ideas in this book have been inspired by the recent work of Dan Sperber and Deirdre Wilson. It has been a privilege to work with Deirdre Wilson during the development of their relevance based theory of pragmatics. However, my gratitude is not just gratitude for her insight and wisdom but also for her constant generosity and understanding.

Finally, I would like to return to the other side of the world and thank my family who, as ever, have kept me going with their encouragement and support.

1
The Domain of Pragmatics

1.1 The Semantics–Pragmatics Distinction

It is generally recognized that the term *meaning* does not describe a single unitary phenomenon. However, the question of how we dissect the meanings of utterances is still the centre of considerable controversy. Nowadays this is usually presented as a controversy over the extent to which *semantic* meaning can be distinguished from *pragmatic* meaning, and the grounds on which such a distinction should be drawn. It might be thought from the title of this book that I believe that such a distinction cannot be maintained: relevance is usually regarded as a pragmatic property, and hence the claim that there are semantic constraints on relevance suggests that semantic meaning and pragmatic interpretation must be part of the same theory. Indeed, I shall argue that relevance is a pragmatic property. Nevertheless, my analysis of certain linguistic expressions as semantic constraints on relevance is based on the assumption that there is a distinction to be drawn – or, more accurately, that a distinction must be drawn. As we shall see, the analysis of these expressions depends on a psychologically adequate account of the role of the context in utterance interpretation, and such an account is possible only given a principled and psychologically grounded distinction between linguistic and non-linguistic knowledge. It is this distinction that I shall argue underlies the distinction between semantics and pragmatics.

This assumption that both semantics and pragmatics should be part of a psychological theory of utterance interpretation distinguishes my approach from the one adopted by, for example,

Gazdar (1979), and not surprisingly it yields a different result.[1] Gazdar's definition of pragmatics is grounded in a particular conception of semantics, a conception which, as we shall see in sections 1.2–3, is not a psychological one. That is, he defines it as 'meaning minus semantics'.

Gazdar's approach to the definition of semantics is in the tradition of Montague,[2] Lewis (1972), and Cresswell (1972). It is a recursive truth definition or, in other words, a means of assigning truth conditions to the sentences of natural language. This means that pragmatics must be defined as the study of all the non-truth-conditional aspects of meaning, or as Gazdar puts it, "Pragmatics = Meaning minus Truth Conditions" (1979: 2). Thus, on this approach pragmatics becomes a means for maintaining the truth-conditional view of semantic meaning in the face of apparent counter-examples. Obviously, one cannot handle counter-examples simply by consigning them to another theoretical level. This would leave us with what Kempson (1975) describes as a pragmatic wastebasket. And, indeed, Gazdar's book aims to give a detailed account of how a pragmatic theory must achieve the goals he has set it. Nevertheless it is worth considering what we would have in our wastebasket given the decision just described.

According to one objection to truth-conditional semantics, we would be left with the interpretation of all non-declarative sentences, for only declarative sentences have truth conditions. On the wastebasket approach, this means that the meanings of the following sentences would have to be studied in pragmatics:

(1) Is Ben coming?
(2) When is Ben coming?
(3) Tell Ben to hurry.
(4) What a delicious meal.

Such sentences have generally been handled in speech-act theory – that is, within the framework of Austin (1962) and Searle (1969). The consignment of such sentences to pragmatics has meant that for many writers (for example, Stalnaker (1972), Bach and Harnish (1979), and Levinson (1983)), speech-act theory is a central part of pragmatics. Since the questions raised by non-declaratives are not central to the main concern of this study, I shall have little to say about the status of speech-act theory in pragmatics. However, the reader may find it interesting to reconsider this objection to truth-conditional semantics in view of my arguments in sections 1.2–3.[3]

Let us turn to the type of case with which Gazdar is primarily concerned. The fact that (6) is generally conveyed by the utterance of (5) might seem to suggest that the natural-language quantifiers are not equivalent to their logical counterparts ∃ and ∀ :

(5) Some of the students were hungry.
(6) Not all of the students were hungry.

However, it will be recognized that (6) is not entailed by (5). The speaker of (5) would not be speaking falsely were (6) to be false. Nor would she be contradicting herself in producing the utterance in (7):

(7) Some, but not all, of the students were hungry.

Significantly, phenomena such as this have been consigned to pragmatics not simply on the grounds that they are non-truth-conditional, but also on the grounds that they can be explained in non-linguistic terms. That is, it is demonstrated that the suggestion in (6) is due not to the meaning of the quantifier *some*, but to general communicative principles. For truth-conditional semanticists this approach, which is due to Grice (1975), has the advantage of allowing the correspondence between the natural-language logical operators and their logical counterparts to be maintained.[4]

In fact, everyday conversation is full of utterances that convey information that is not part of their truth-conditional content. Consider for example, the exchange in (8):

(8) A: Would you like a chocolate?
     B: I'm on a diet.

B's reply will normally be understood to convey the information in (9):

(9) I would not like a chocolate.

However, no-one would accuse her of lying were she to take a chocolate. Nor would anyone want to say that the sentence she uttered means that she wouldn't like a chocolate. Uttered in another situation it may not convey this information at all. As we shall see in section 1.5, phenomena such as this have become the central concern of Gricean pragmatics. However, it seems that they are of less concern to formal pragmatists like Gazdar who have preferred to concentrate on the type of phenomenon illustrated in (5)–(6) above. The point here is that whereas the suggestion in (6) can be dealt with by setting up a general rule associating (5) with its pragmatic interpretation (6) and then effectively blocking its application in contexts where (6) is known to be false, the suggestion in (9) is due to an idiosyncratic feature of the context and cannot, therefore, be predicted by a general rule. Since Gazdar is interested in establishing a formal procedure by which pragmatic interpretations are assigned to utterances (analogous to the formal procedure by which truth conditions are assigned to sentences), one would not expect phenomena such as the suggestion in (9) to feature in his theory.

At this point it would seem that the truth-conditional/non-truth-conditional distinction corresponds to the linguistic/non-linguistic distinction. However, this is not the case. As is well known, there are many examples of linguistic meaning which cannot be defined truth-conditionally. For example, many semanticists would regard each of the following as having identical truth conditions:

(10)(a)   It was Susan who hit Tom.
   (b)   It was Tom whom Susan hit.

Yet surely the fact that these sentences would be interpreted differently is due to the difference in their word order. A similar point can be made about (11) (a) and (b), where the difference in interpretation is due to the meaning of *but*:

(11)(a)   Susan has passed her exam and I'm very pleased.
   (b)   Susan has passed her exam but I'm very pleased.

These are the type of phenomena most central to the goals of this book, and we shall be considering many more examples in later chapters. My most immediate concern here is to discuss, first, the extent to which such phenomena are a serious counter-example to truth-conditional semantics, and, second, the extent to which their inclusion in the pragmatic wastebasket is justified. Basically, my argument will be that the view that the existence of such words and constructions is a threat to truth-conditional semantics results from the mistaken assumption that natural-language sentences have truth conditions, and that their inclusion in pragmatics leads to the conflation of linguistic and non-linguistic meaning, a position which is undesirable in a psychological theory of utterance interpretation.

If natural-language sentences had truth conditions, then we ought to be able to specify the conditions under which the following sentences are true:

(12) I arrived today.
(13) Nellie tripped over her trunk.
(14) That is hot.
(15) Everyone was.

But of course this is not possible. We cannot assign truth conditions to these sentences unless we have more information. In the case of (12) we have to know the identity of the speaker and the time of utterance. In (13) we have to know, in addition to the time of utterance, who or what the referent of *Nellie* is and what sense of the word *trunk* was intended. For (14) we need to know what is being referred to and what sense of *hot* was intended; and for (15) we have to know what the domain of the quantifier is and what property is being predicated. Notice that this information is information not about sentences, but about utterances of sentences. That is, it is about the particular use of a sentence, by a particular speaker on a particular occasion. In other words, it seems that truth conditions are assigned only to sentence-context pairs.

It was in response to this sort of problem that formal semanticists like Montague and Lewis developed an enriched version of their truth-conditional programme, a programme which Montague himself referred to as pragmatics. As we shall see in section 1.2, this solution to the problem of context is hardly adequate as a psychological theory of the way utterances are understood. In fact, it does not attempt to deal with any other cases of context dependence beyond that exhibited by utterances containing deictic or indexical expressions (for instance, *today*, *I*, *that*, *here*). And even here it seriously underestimates the difference between the questions raised by the use of non-linguistic knowledge in the interpretation of utterances and the role of linguistic or grammatical knowledge.

However, Gazdar accepts that the formal truth-conditional treatment of deictic expressions is adequate, which means that given his definition of pragmatics as "meaning minus truth conditions", he must exclude the interpretation of deictic expressions from its domain. This conflation of linguistically determined meaning and contextually determined meaning is justified – indeed necessary – for him on the grounds that since indexical expressions permeate natural language, the adoption of Montague's terminology would mean that "natural languages will have only a syntax and a pragmatics" (1979: 2). But as we shall see, it is simply inappropriate to think of a natural language 'having' a semantics, if this is defined as a theory of the way truth conditions are assigned, let alone 'having' a pragmatics.

1.2 Indexical Semantics

Gazdar's decision to exclude deixis, or the interpretation of indexical expressions, from the domain of pragmatics is based on the assumption that this is "standardly and naturally handled with truth conditional apparatus" (1979: 2). A similar assumption is made by Levinson (1983), who adds that this study could be considered part of semantics by a different criterion: "The many facets of deixis are so pervasive in natural languages, and so deeply grammaticalised, that it is hard to think of them as anything other than an essential part of semantics" (1983: 55). To be fair to Levinson, he also goes on to add that since deixis concerns the relationship between linguistic expressions and the contexts in which they are used, according to some criteria it should be studied in pragmatics. Nevertheless it is clear that the reasons that led Levinson to include deixis in his book are different from those that led him to include conversational implicature. For according to his account, there is no role for the general pragmatic principles or maxims that he invokes in his account of implicature in an account of the interpretation of deixis.

As I mentioned in section 1.1, formal semanticists have not ignored the fact that the truth values of utterances containing indexical expressions cannot be determined independently of the context. Moreover, it is clear that the contextual features that must be taken into account are determined by the grammatical properties of the indexical expressions used. Thus, for example, the time adverbials *in 30 seconds* and *yesterday* in (16)(a) and (c) show that the time of utterance must be taken into account, while in (16)(b) the use of *here* indicates that the hearer must take into account the place of utterance. The demonstratives *this* and *that* are used to indicate non-human objects in the context; the value of *you* in (16)(c) must be the hearer, and the value of *I* in (16)(b) must be the speaker:

(16)(a)   This will explode in 30 seconds.
   (b)   I brought it over here.
   (c)   You bought that yesterday.

However, while the truth-conditional apparatus mentioned by Gazdar makes provision for the fact that context dependence is encoded in the grammatical properties of utterances, it is not clear that it provides an explanation for the way such utterances are actually interpreted.

According to the standard truth-conditional view, the meaning of a sentence is defined in terms of the set of possible worlds in which it is true. The idea behind the introduction of possible worlds is basically that there are various respects in which the world could have been different from the way that in fact it is, so that saying that a sentence like *Grass is green* is true in saying that our world is one of a set of possible worlds in which grass is green. Alternatively, one might say that the meaning of this sentence is a function which takes a possible world as an argument and yields a truth value. In order to account for the fact that the truth value of a sentence containing *I* or *today* depends on the context, it is suggested that we simply need to include in our semantic description not just a specification of possible worlds, but also a specification of the context. Thus for example, if we include the information that the speaker is Diane and that today is 5 April 1986, then we shall know that (17) is true in those worlds in which Diane arrived on 5 April 1986.

(17)   I arrived today. (= (12))

On this approach a context is simply a set or an *index* of coordinates for speakers, addressees, times of utterance, places of utterance, indicated objects, and whatever else is needed. What is needed is, of course, determined by the grammatical properties of the utterance. Thus the use of the past tense in (16)(b) and (c) means that a time of utterance co-ordinate will be needed, and the use of a demonstrative such as *this* or *that* shows that an indicated objects co-ordinate will be required, and so on. Now, in the case just discussed the grammatical properties of the sentence are such that the hearer is directed to a unique context and, hence, a unique interpretation. *I* means 'the speaker' and *yesterday* means 'the day prior to this' and in both cases there will only be one referent meeting this description on any given occasion. However, when we turn to sentences containing expressions like *this* and *that* we have a problem deciding what information should be included in the index, for on any given occasion of utterance there is invariably more than one object that the speaker could have intended. Even pointing does not always resolve the question. Consider, for example, how you would interpret the following two utterances made by a speaker pointing to a carton of orange juice:

(18) This is good for you.
(19) This is made from trees.

A similar problem arises in the case of *here*. One assumes that the interpretation of an utterance containing this word requires a specification of the place where the speaker is located. However, the grammatical properties of such an utterance cannot specify the boundaries of that place. That is, it is not clear whether the speaker of (16)(b) is saying that she brought it into the room from which she is speaking or some larger place that includes that room. The actual interpretation will depend on a number of factors which cannot be predicted from the grammatical properties of the utterance – for example, on whether the speaker is talking about a car or a book.

Obviously, there are many other respects in which the propositional (that is, truth-conditional) content of an utterance is left unspecified by its grammatical properties: indexical semantics does not attempt to deal with the role of the context in disambiguation or in the recovery of ellipsed or otherwise unexpressed material.

My point here, however, is that even its concern with the interpretation of indexicals is restricted by its inability to specify anything more than a range of grammatically possible interpretations.

At this point a proponent of formal semantics might object that the task of explaining how contexts are actually selected and thus how utterances are actually understood is not a task for semantics, but for pragmatics. Certainly, this is not a task for semantics as it is conceived by, for example, Lewis (1972). For according to this conception, semantics is concerned with language as an abstract system in which symbols are associated with aspects of the world, and not with the use of that system by any person or population. The extension of this purely formal machinery to include the interpretation of context-dependent expressions is in the same non-psychological spirit. Thus, as we have seen, the context is defined objectively, independently of speaker or hearer, as the set of individuals, times, places, etc. that supply the values of the variable expressions. Obviously, the problem of context selection could only be addressed by a theory that aimed to explain how hearers use their beliefs and assumptions in the interpretation of utterances.

Thus the criticism that indexical semantics does not provide an account of the way that contexts are selected amounts to a claim that formal semanticists have not attempted to provide a psychological theory of utterance interpretation. Is this criticism justified? It is clear that the formal semantics programme proceeds from an interest in what Chomsky (1986) has called *E-languages* (that is, external languages or sets of sentences) rather than the *I-languages* or internalized grammars underlying those E-languages. However, Chomsky argues that it is impossible to study an E-language without making some assumption about the I-language underlying it. Since the E-language with which semanticists like Lewis are concerned is natural language, this means that their purely formalist methodology is inappropriate. In particular, it means that it is not legitimate to propose a theory of the interpretation of context-dependent expressions that does not attempt to address the problem of how contexts are determined.

Lewis (1972) does, however, address this problem when he considers the interpretation of definite descriptions. "Consider the sentence 'The door is open'. This does not mean that the one and only door that now exists is open; nor does it mean that the one and only door near the place of utterance, or pointed at is open" (1972: 214). What the speaker means, says Lewis, is that the one and only door among the objects that are somehow prominent on the occasion of utterance is open. Accordingly, he introduces a new contextual index, a *prominent objects co-ordinate*, which is intended to specify which of all the objects satisfying a particular definite description are contextually prominent or salient.

Lewis evidently regards this simply as an extension of the machinery of indexical semantics. However, in introducing this co-ordinate he is clearly admitting the need for a psychological definition of context. As Lewis himself says, the interpretation of a definite description must depend on mental factors such as the speaker's expectations regarding the objects she is likely to bring to the attention of her audience. But given that judgements about the salience of objects vary from person to person – that is, they are subjective – it is difficult to see how a speaker could expect her audience to select the context that is in accordance with her intentions.

Notice, too, that contextual prominence is not sufficient for ensuring the correct choice of context for the assignment of reference. For example, in (20) (adapted from Maclaran 1982) both the entities referred to by *Periah's recording of the Moonlight Sonata* and *the Moonlight Sonata* are made accessible to the hearer. However, this does not ensure that the correct reference is assigned to each of the two identical pronouns:

(20) A: Have you heard Periah's recording of the Moonlight Sonata?
     B: Yes, it made me realize I'd never be able to play it.

That is, there is no way of specifying which of two equally salient objects is the one intended by the speaker.

The assumption underlying Lewis's (1972) proposals seems to be that the hearer selects a context and then uses it in recovering the intended interpretation. However, it is not at all clear that hearers actually follow this procedure. Indeed, as Lewis points out in a later paper (1979), in many cases the hearer selects the context on the basis of certain assumptions about what the speaker's intentions actually are. The main claim of Lewis's paper is that the kinematics of salience are governed by a rule of accommodation which requires the hearer to adjust the comparative salience of an object in order to accommodate her assumption that an utterance is acceptable. Lewis's example concerns two cats, one of which has gained maximal salience over the course of the conversation. If the next utterance referring to a cat is false or otherwise unacceptable when this cat continues to be understood as the most salient cat, then the hearer must regard the other cat as having maximal salience and hence as the one intended by the speaker.

It is difficult to see how this rule could be, as Lewis suggests, just one of the rules determining the hearer's choice of context. No matter how salient an object is according to any other criterion, it will be included in the range of possible values for a referring expression only if this is compatible with the assumption that the utterance is acceptable. If this is right, then the context for the interpretation of an utterance cannot be fixed in advance, as Lewis's earlier account seemed to suggest, but rather must be constructed as part of the process of interpreting it.

While Lewis's rule of accommodation captures this important point about the selection of contextual information, it is too vague to provide the basis for a complete theory of utterance interpretation. Obviously, the hearer's aim is to bring to bear the contextual information that yields an acceptable interpretation of the utterance. However, unless we are able to specify the conditions under which an utterance is acceptable we shall not be able to say what the hearer's goal in selecting and using the context for its interpretation is. As we shall see in the next section, this question takes us not only out of the domain of the abstract semantic system described by Lewis in 'General Semantics', but also beyond the scope of a psychologically real grammar.

1.3 Linguistic and Non-Linguistic Knowledge

The arguments so far might seem to suggest that truth-conditional semantics should apply not to sentences, but to utterances. That is, truth conditions are assigned to a particular use of a sentence, in a particular context. As we saw in the previous section, the fact that the context plays a role in determining the truth-conditional content of utterances means that there can be no purely formal mechanism for assigning semantic interpretations. We need to take account of the psychological constraints that govern the hearer's choice of context for the interpretation of a given utterance. In this section I wish to show that the questions raised by the role of the context in utterance interpretation apply to all human information-processing and, therefore, belong not to the theory of grammar or even to a theory of communication, but to a general theory of human cognition.

Within the framework of generative grammar it is assumed that certain sound sequences are assigned various levels of representation – phonological, syntactic, and logical – which are related to each other by a system of linguistic rules or computations. While this system of rules and representations provides the basis for the (propositional) knowledge that such and such a sound sequence is or is not a grammatical sentence of the language in question, it cannot itself be characterized in terms of a set of propositional knowledge statements. A grammatical representation is a representation of a sound sequence – the sound sequence that caused it. However, the existence of that sound sequence could not be said to make that representation true or false. As Chomsky puts it, "The question of truth, conformity to an external reality does not enter in the way that it does in connection with our knowledge of the properties of objects" (1980: 27).

This has led some philosophers to criticize Chomsky for talking of knowledge of language at all. Certainly, knowledge of the rules and representations of grammar could not be described as justified, true belief. However, as Chomsky (1980) points out, this traditional definition of knowledge itself receives little support either from ordinary usage or from general epistemological considerations.[5] This debate aside, it is clear that knowledge of grammar cannot be reduced to knowing how, to a set of behavioural dispositions. It crucially involves a system of mental representations and computations. If the fact that these representations are not truth-bearing conceptual representations and the computations performed over them are not truth-preserving computations disqualifies them from being known, then we could follow Chomsky's suggestion and use the term *cognise* instead.

Nevertheless, it is clear that this system of rules and representations provides a means for acquiring conceptual representations

– that is, for acquiring assumptions about possible or actual states of affairs. A means, but not, of course, the means. Assumptions about the world are acquired not only through natural language, but also through the various perceptual systems. Thus, for example, I may be told that it is raining or I may discover it for myself. Either way the assumption I acquire may be true or it may be false. That is, either way the representation I acquire has truth conditions.

This distinction that is emerging here plays a central role in the modular approach to human cognition according to which the mind is regarded as a variety of specialized systems individuated by virtue of their computational properties. In particular, it underlies the distinction drawn by J. A. Fodor (1983a) between two broad types of system: the input systems, which process visual, auditory, linguistic, and other perceptual information; and the central systems which integrate the input from the various perceptual sources with background information stored in memory, performing inferences on it, and arriving at conclusions about the world.

Fodor argues that each input system is *modular*: that is, it has its own method of representation and computation, and can only process information with the properties for which its computations are defined. Thus, for example, the visual system can only process visual information (distal layouts), the auditory system can only process acoustic information, and the computations of the grammar are defined over representations with certain formal properties. In particular, none of these systems can have access to the full range of propositional or conceptual representations stored in memory, or, as Fodor puts it, they are "informationally encapsulated". Central systems, by contrast, are modality neutral: they integrate and perform inferences on information derived from all the input systems and from memory.

The fact that the computations of the central system of thought are inferential means that they must be defined for representations with semantic (that is, truth-conditional) properties. An inference is distinguished from other computations by the fact that it is truth-preserving: given true propositions as input it will yield a true proposition as output. This suggests that there must be some means for getting the non-propositional representations of the grammar or perceptual systems into a propositional form, or, in other words, some means of constructing propositional hypotheses on the basis of the grammar which can then be tested by the central processes in the light of background information stored in memory. But, as Fodor points out, the process of hypothesis formation and confirmation is very poorly understood. Indeed, it is not clear that it ever could be understood at all. The problem is that in principle there is no limit to either the number of hypotheses that might be considered or the number of items on background information that might turn out to have a bearing on the confirmation of a particular hypothesis. ". . . the reason that there is no serious psychology of central processes is the same reason there is no serious philosophy of scientific confirmation: both exemplify the significance of global factors in the fixation of belief, and nobody begins to understand how such factors have their effects" (1983a: 140).

It is significant here that Fodor takes scientific-theory construction as the most typical example of the operation of the central system of thought. If he is right and whatever applies to scientific fixation of belief applies to all other examples of fixation of belief, then the call for a psychological theory of utterance interpretation made in section 1.2 is unrealistic.

However, as Sperber and Wilson (1986) have pointed out, it is not clear that scientific theorizing is in fact the most typical model of a cognitive process. Certainly, it is not clear that it is the most appropriate model for the cognitive processes involved in utterance interpretation. The construction and confirmation of a scientific theory may take place over a very long time, and hence an enormous number of hypotheses may be considered and any amount of evidence may be brought to bear. In contrast, utterance interpretation is, in general, almost instantaneous. Hearers rarely spend days, let alone months or years, working out the interpretation of an utterance or text. While, logically speaking, any number of hypotheses might be considered and any amount of background information brought to bear, the hearer's choice of hypothesis and evidence is constrained by psychological factors, in particular, by her desire to minimize the amount of processing required for the recovery of relevant information. Consequently, her choice of hypothesis and evidence will be restricted to the ones that are most immediately accessible. Notice too that given that a speaker wishes to communicate with a hearer, it follows that she will generally co-operate by making the comprehension task easier – for example, by making the relevant background information accessible. Scientific data are not, of course, derived from a co-operative source.

Sperber and Wilson's programme forms the backbone of this study, and we shall be seeing how the ideas just outlined can be developed into an overall pragmatic theory in the next chapter. Right now, however, let us consider the implications of the foregoing discussion for the questions raised at the beginning of the present chapter. First, notice that if semantic theory is defined as a theory of the way truth conditions are assigned, then it cannot be a part of the grammar. As we have seen, the recovery of a propositional or conceptual representation from the utterance of a sentence requires non-linguistic or world knowledge. To extend the grammar so that it can take account of such knowledge would be to include a component with intensional properties along with a component with purely formal properties. If we regard grammatical knowledge as a module, it is difficult to see why one bit of it should have a set of computational properties (e.g. truth-conditional ones) lacking in the other bit. Moreover, if we regard utterance interpretation as exemplifying the cognitive processes involved in the acquisition of belief from other sources, then it is difficult to see why those processes should be described in a theory whose domain is restricted to language use. In particular, it is difficult to see why the general cognitive principles that constrain the hearer's choice of context should be regarded as part of the grammar.

Does this mean, as Gazdar suggested it would, that natural languages do not have a semantics? So far I have been using the term *semantic* to describe the properties, not of natural language sentences, but of sentences in what Fodor (1976) calls the language of thought. However, this terminological decision does not reflect the fact that while linguistic expressions may not have truth conditions, there is still a sense in which they have meanings. For example, in section 1.2 we appealed to the meanings of *I*, *this*, and *today*, the point being that these meanings did not determine a complete proposition, but only a blueprint for a proposition. Such blueprints have been called *logical forms*. Thus we might say that a theory of linguistic semantics must provide a specification of the rules that translate natural-language sentences into logical forms.[6]

This suggests that we have isolated three separate enterprises: (i) The translation of natural-language sentences into logical forms; (ii) the determination of propositional content on the basis of the context; and (iii) the assignment of truth conditions to propositions or thoughts. In other words, it would seem that we do not have a simple bifurcation of meaning as was suggested in my opening remarks. However, recall that my aim was to distinguish semantics and pragmatics in a psychological theory of utterance interpretation. According to the arguments of this section, while (i) and (ii) are not both part of grammar, they are nevertheless both part of a psychological theory. What about the enterprise in (iii)?

Within this framework propositions are not simply abstract entities with logical properties. They also have psychological properties. That is, they are representations which undergo mental processes. As we have seen, these mental processes are distinguished from other computations by the fact that they are truth-preserving, or, in other words, that they are defined for representations which describe the state of affairs, actual or possible, which would make them true. Clearly, if the descriptions of these states of affairs (or truth conditions) were themselves represented as psychological entities, then the conceptual representations that are taken as input to inference rules would not be representations of anything in the external world, which would mean that they would not have the properties for which these computations are defined.

Moreover, saying that truth conditions were psychologically real would mean that they would play a role in mental processes. As Fodor has argued in his paper 'Methodological Solipsism' (in Fodor 1981a), this is not the case: the inferences we perform may be truth-preserving, but these inferences are not affected by the semantic (or intensional) properties of the representations that they take as input. Consider for example, the much discussed inference in (21):

(21)(a) Copernicus believed that Venus is a planet.
    (b) Venus = the Evening Star.
    (c) Therefore Copernicus believed that the Evening Star is a planet.

As is well known, this inference is invalid, a fact generally attributed to the fact that the first premise involves a belief operator, or, in other word, that the verb *believe* creates an opaque context. Fodor takes this opacity as evidence for the psychological unreality of truth-conditional semantics. The point is that Copernicus's belief represents the state of affairs that would make it true. As it happens, this state of affairs is identical to one that would make a different thought (that is, a different propositional form) true. But since this state of affairs is not in Copernicus's head, it is not going to play any role in any inferences he makes. The only thing that can be taken as input to any inferences he performs is his belief that Venus is a planet. Notice that, according to this account, thoughts or conceptual representations are individuated by virtue of their form rather than of their content. The suggestion, then, is that while inferential computations are truth-preserving, they only have access to the formal (or syntactic) properties of the representations they take as input.

If these arguments are right, then the enterprise (iii), above, cannot be included in a theory of human cognition. Indeed, to include it in this theory would be to undermine the coherence of the cognitive framework which, as we have seen, underlies the enterprise in (ii). This means that within a purely psychological framework the only contrast that we have is between (i) and (ii) – that is, between linguistic semantics and the theory of the principles governing the use of contextual information in interpretation. Accordingly, in this study the semantics–pragmatics contrast corresponds to the distinction between linguistic knowledge and non-linguistic knowledge.

It will be recalled that the main concern of this study is with a class of phenomena that have often been regarded as counter-examples to truth-conditional theories of semantics. Clearly, the existence of linguistic expressions and constructions that have meanings that cannot be defined truth-conditionally is a serious objection to the view that sentences have truth conditions. But we have just seen that sentences do not have truth conditions. If linguistic semantics (i) above is not directly truth-conditional, then there is no reason to think that every aspect of linguistic meaning is definable in truth-conditional terms. Nevertheless the existence of these words does have implications for linguistic semantics as it is defined in (i). For according to this definition, linguistic semantics is concerned with logical forms, and I have defined logical forms as blueprints for propositions. The problem is that the expressions with which I shall be concerned play no part at all in the determination of propositional content, and hence cannot be regarded as part of logical form. Yet we would want to say that these expressions do contribute to the interpretation of the utterances that contain them, and hence that they have meaning.

As we shall see in chapter 2, pragmatic interpretation does not just involve the recovery of propositional content: the hearer is also expected to assess the impact of the proposition on her existing representation of the world. The goal of this study is to show that the meanings of those expressions that do not play a role in determining the proposition expressed by the utterances that contain them should be analysed in terms of constraints on the inferential computations the hearer performs in order to establish the impact of that proposition – or, in other words, its relevance. In other words, not all linguistic meaning can be defined solely in terms of input to the processes that deliver propositional representations of the world. Some linguistic meaning actually provides an instruction as to the way in which the proposition recovered is to be processed for relevance.

1.4 Pragmatics and the Competence–Performance Distinction

Pragmatic theory, from the point of view of this study, is the theory of the mental structure underlying the ability to interpret utterances in context. In the previous section we saw that this structure can be distinguished from the structure underlying grammatical competence by the character (and hence the domain) of the computations it involves. Now we turn to the question of whether, or in what sense, the possession of this structure can be regarded as pragmatic competence. This question is prompted by the controversy between those linguists (for example, Kempson 1975) who have argued that pragmatics is an aspect of linguistic performance, and those (for example, Gazdar 1979) who claim that pragmatic theory must be 'competencist'. The problem here is that the terms *competence* and *performance* may be understood in a number of different ways, and while there is a sense in which Kempson's view is correct, there is another sense – although not, I believe, the one intended by Gazdar – in which we must speak of a theory of pragmatic competence.

In this study I take the competence–performance distinction to be an example of the kind of idealization required for the explanation of any phenomenon that is the result of more than one factor. Actual linguistic behaviour is the result of a number of factors, some psychological, some sociological, some universal, some tied to some particular experience. In order to achieve an understanding of any one of these factors it is essential to suspend our knowledge of – or even our interest in – the others, or, in other words, to abstract away from them. I shall argue that pragmatics must be regarded as part of linguistic performance to the extent that it is not part of grammatical competence. On the other hand, abstracting away from grammatical competence leaves us with a whole range of phenomena not all of which we would want to call pragmatic. In particular, we are left with phenomena that are the result of social factors and ones that are the result of limitations of memory and attention. These phenomena are not explained in terms of the mental structures underlying the fixation of belief, but rather in terms of the sociolinguistic and psycholinguistic factors that affect the employment of this structure. The point here is that pragmatic theory itself involves idealization: the computational structure it characterizes can be studied independently of the use of this structure in specific circumstances – just as the mental structure underlying grammatical competence can be studied independently of the factors that affect its use on a particular occasion. Chomsky's term "pragmatic competence" (1980: 224) is, I believe, intended to reflect the fact that this kind of idealization is involved, and not that pragmatics is an extension of grammatical competence (cf. Gazdar 1979).

The suggestion that pragmatic theory involves abstracting away from the particular properties of the situation in which it is put to use is not meant to conflict with the generally accepted view that pragmatics is the study of utterances or sentences in use. The whole point of pragmatic theory is to explain how the context is used in the interpretation of utterances. However, the general principles that govern the hearer's selection and use of background beliefs underlie behaviour which may also be affected by factors independent of the knowledge of those principles. For example, it has been mentioned that the hearer's aim in interpreting an utterance is to recover relevant information about the world at a minimum cost in processing. Clearly, the amount of effort a hearer is actually prepared to spend on the interpretation of an utterance will vary according to the situation she is in: she might, for instance, be prepared to put more effort into extracting information from a remark made in a lecture than she would into the interpretation of a remark made during a leisurely chat over dinner. Moreover, what one person regards as a reasonable amount of effort in a given situation may be regarded as unreasonable by another. Finally, the amount of effort that any one person actually puts into the interpretation of an utterance depends on how tired she is, how much she has had to drink, and so on. It would, perhaps, be interesting to study the effect of these factors on actual linguistic behaviour. However, this is not the task of a pragmatic theory, for while they may affect the way that the hearer puts her knowledge of pragmatic principles to use, they do not affect the mental structure in terms of which this knowledge must be analysed.

The same point can be made about the factors that determine the structure of a particular belief set or context. The fact that the hearer is trying to minimize processing costs means that she will bring only the most accessible of her background beliefs to bear on the interpretation of an utterance. The structure of a hearer's belief set is determined by a variety of factors. But while it is essential that a pragmatic theory should recognize that belief sets are structured by degrees of accessibility, it is not its task to predict the actual structure, or, indeed, the content of any one hearer's belief set. Interestingly, the structure of a hearer's belief set is often determined by the speaker's use of certain grammatical devices that focus on a particular subset of his beliefs. While these devices interact with general pragmatic principles for their effect, their specification lies outside the domain of pragmatics and within that of grammar. This means that their study belongs to the study of grammatical, rather than pragmatic, competence. However, as I have indicated, the explanation of their role must be grounded in a theory of the effect of the context in utterance interpretation. Let us, then, turn to the question of how such a theory might be formulated.

1.5 Grice's Theory of Conversation

In his 1967 William James Lectures (Grice 1975) Grice advocated a view of verbal communication which has had a profound influence on pragmatic theorizing. His basic idea was that in communicating speakers aim to conform to certain general principles or maxims – the maxims of truthfulness, informativeness, relevance, and clarity – and that hearers interpret utterances with these principles in mind. On this approach, utterance interpretation is not a matter of encoding and decoding messages, but rather involves taking the meaning of the sentence uttered together with contextual information and inference rules, and working out what the speaker meant on the basis of the assumption that the utterance conforms to very general principles of conversation.

The main advantage of this approach from Grice's point of view was that it allowed him to maintain a parsimonious semantics by providing a non-semantic (or pragmatic) explanation for a wide range of phenomena which had hitherto posed serious problems for traditional, truth-conditional theories of meaning. In particular, he aimed to provide a pragmatic account of the non-truth-functional senses which ordinary language philosophers had been attributing to the natural-language connectives – for example, the temporal connotations of *and* in utterances like (22), or the suggestion conveyed by the use of *or* in (23) that the speaker does not know which of the disjuncts is true:

(22) He ran over to the window and jumped.
(23) He either jumped out of the window or fell.

More generally, he wished to avoid positing a large number of divergent, but related, senses for words in accordance with a principle which he describes as a modified version of Occam's Razor: "Senses are not to be multiplied beyond necessity" (1978: 118–19). Thus he distinguished between *what is said* – that is, those aspects of the total meaning of an utterance which can be attributed to linguistic knowledge – and *what is implicated* – that is, those aspects of meaning that are due to the interaction of linguistic meaning with general communicative principles.

For example, according to his account, what the speaker says in uttering (22) is simply its truth-conditional content – the conjunction of the propositions in (24):

(24)(a) He ran over to the window.
   (b) He jumped.

The suggestion that he jumped after he ran over to the window is an implicature due to the assumption that the utterance conforms to the Maxim of Manner which, amongst other things, requires speakers to be orderly – or, in other words, to describe events in the order in which they occurred.[7] Notice that the implicated part of the message can be cancelled without contradiction:

(25) She made a pot of tea and fed the cat, but not necessarily in that order.
(26) The prize is either in the garden or in the attic. I know that because I know where I put it.

(Grice 1978: 116)

However, while this shows that the suggestion is pragmatically determined, it is not necessarily the case that it is not part of the propositional (or truth-conditional) content of the utterance. Indeed as Cohen (1971) has pointed out, the fact that the temporal and causal connotations of conjoined utterances may fall under the scope of logical operators such as *if . . . then*, *or*, and negation suggests that they must. I shall postpone discussion of Cohen's examples to a later chapter when the interpretation of conjoined utterances is considered in more detail.[8] In the meantime let us consider some rather less controversial examples of the way in which Grice's distinction between 'what is said' and 'what is implicated' has led to the conflation of linguistic meaning and propositional (or truth-conditional) semantics.

Grice himself did not use the term *pragmatic*.[9] Nevertheless, it seems that he was trying to provide a general framework into which every aspect of utterance interpretation can be accommodated, and that all aspects of the total meaning of an utterance belong either to what is said or to what is implicated. This has led a number of his followers (for example, Gazdar (1979), Karttunen

(1974)) to construe his notion of what is said as being coextensive with truth-conditional semantics and his notion of conversational implicature as the key notion in the explanation of non-truth-conditional – or pragmatic phenomena. According to this interpretation, the domain of semantics consists of linguistically specified, truth-conditional phenomena, while that of pragmatics consists of non-linguistic, non-truth-conditional aspects of interpretation, a view which, as we have seen, does not take into account the extent to which pragmatic principles may play a role in the determination of the propositional content of utterances.

As Grice himself pointed out, knowing what the speaker actually said in producing a particular utterance is a matter of, first, knowing what range of possible senses and possible referents could have been intended, and, second, knowing which sense and reference was intended on that occasion. In section 1.1 we saw that while the meanings of the words uttered may determine the first, they cannot determine the second. That is, B's response in (27) has two possible senses, depending on whether *hot* means 'warm' or 'spicy', and an indefinite range of possible referents, since *it* could refer to any object known to the hearer:

(27)   A: You're not eating.
       B: It's too hot.

Similarly, to take an example adapted from Wilson and Sperber, (28) has two possible senses, depending on whether *admit* means 'let in' or 'confess to', and an indefinite range of possible referents for *them*:

(28)   I refused to admit them.

However, when it is produced in response to (29), the hearer can immediately eliminate all the possible interpretations except for the one in which *admit* means 'confess to' and *them* refers to the speaker's mistakes:

(29)   What did you do when you make mistakes?

Obviously, A's utterance in (27) does not provide such an unequivocal contextual clue as to the actual interpretation of B's. However, it will at least be evident to the hearer that *it* refers either to the food or to the weather, and not to any other inanimate object the hearer may know of.

Wilson and Sperber's point is that whatever the context of these utterances, they still have an indefinite range of linguistically possible interpretations, any one of which could have been intended by a speaker who was not observing the conversational maxims. However, as Grice himself pointed out, hearers interpret utterances on the assumption that the maxims have been observed. It will be assumed, for example, that the speaker of (28) in the context of (29) is being relevant. This will lead to the elimination of any interpretation in which *admit* means 'let in' and *them* refers to anything other than the speaker's mistakes. That is, it will lead to the elimination of any interpretation not consistent with the assumption that the relevance maxim has been observed. In other words, the sense and reference to an utterance is not fully determined by semantic rules, but is pragmatically determined by the context and by the maxim of relevance.

If this is right, then the distinction between what is said and what is implicated cannot be coextensive with the distinction between semantics and pragmatics: pragmatics must be concerned not just with the implicated suggestions conveyed by an utterance, but also with the implicit aspects of its propositional content. As Wilson and Sperber point out, the pragmatically determined aspects of propositional content are not exhausted by disambiguation and the ascription of reference. Utterances are frequently elliptical or fragmentary: consider such everyday utterances as 'Telephone' or 'Any letters?'. And yet in every case the hearer is expected to recover a complete proposition. Further, there are cases in which the meaning of the words uttered does determine a proposition which, although complete, is too underspecified to be taken as the one the speaker could have intended. Consider, for example, the utterances in (30) (from Wilson and Sperber 1981) and (31) (from Carston 1985):

(30) John plays well.
(31) It will take us some time to get there.

Play is ambiguous between 'play a musical instrument' and 'play a game'. As we have just seen, a hearer presented with (30) in a particular context, say, the one in which John Smith is playing the violin, will be able to ascribe a particular sense and reference to it – that is, the one represented in (32):

(32)   John Smith plays a musical instrument well.

However, Wilson and Sperber point out that in this context the assumption that the Relevance Maxim has been observed will lead the hearer to recover a more completely specified proposition – that is, the one in (33):

(33)   John Smith plays the violin well.

In principle, the hearer of (31) could recover a complete proposition on the basis of its linguistic content together with reference assignment. However, she would not thereby recover anything she didn't know already: obviously the event of going to a location takes place over time. In this case, the hearer's assumption that the utterance conforms to the Maxim of Informativeness will lead her to recover a much more completely specified proposition – for example, the one in (34):

(34)   It will take longer to get there than you think.

Within Grice's framework, information whose recovery depends on the conversational maxims is part of what is implicated rather than what is said. If we wanted to maintain this definition of an implicature, then we would have to say that the propositions in (33) and (34) and the results of disambiguation and reference assignment should be classified as part of *what is implicated*, and that *what is said* should be restricted to the range of possible meanings specified by the grammar. Clearly, this is inconsistent with Grice's original intention. Moreover, it undermines what pragmatists have regarded as the most intuitively appealing contribution of his theory of implicature – namely, that it provides an account of how it is possible to convey more than just the explicit propositional content of an utterance. To illustrate, recall Grice's example of the speaker who, on meeting a man walking along the road carrying an empty petrol can, produces the utterance in (35):

(35)   There's a garage around the corner.

In addition to the information that there is a garage around the corner the hearer of this utterance will immediately recover the information in (36):

(36) I can obtain petrol around the corner.

However, (36) would not be regarded as part of the truth-conditional content of (35): the speaker could not be accused of having spoken falsely had there been no petrol obtainable around the corner. It is simply a proposition that follows from (35) given certain other assumptions, for example, the assumption that the garage is open or that it sells petrol.

Given that we do wish to distinguish between the propositional content of an utterance and the implications or suggestions that can be worked out on the basis of that content together with the context, then it would seem that instead of distinguishing between what is said and what is implicated we distinguish between the proposition the speaker is taken to have expressed (the truth-conditional content of the utterance) and the implications that follow from it. Grice was right to show that the suggestions that a hearer recovers from an utterance over and above its propositional content are recovered on the basis of the context together with general communicative principles. The hearer of (35) would only recover the proposition in (36) if he assumed that the speaker was being informative and relevant. Moreover, Grice's followers were correct to construe his theory of implicature as the basis of a pragmatic theory. However, neither Grice nor his followers recognized that the effects of pragmatic principles extend to the determination of propositional content.[10]

It is not surprising, then, that we do not find Gricean accounts of the problems of context selection associated with the indexical phenomena discussed in section 1.4 above. Unfortunately, however, Grice's account does not provide a solution to this problem as it arises in the interpretation of implicatures either. Although he recognized that background or contextual assumptions play a role in the recovery of implicatures, he said nothing about how the appropriate assumptions are selected or about what role they play. Consider, for example, the exchange in (37).

(37) A: Are you going to the talk this afternoon?
B: It's on phonetics.

The Domain of Pragmatics   27

A hearer who interprets B's reply on the basis of the contextual assumption in (38)(a) will take her to be implicating the proposition in (38(b), while a hearer who supplies the assumption in (39)(a) will recover the proposition in (39)(b):

(38)(a)   B never misses a talk on phonetics.
   (b)   B is going to the talk this afternoon.
(39)(a)   B never goes to phonetics talks.
   (b)   B is not going to the talk this afternoon.

Of course, in principle, the hearer of (37)(b) could bring any of her accessible beliefs and assumptions to bear on the interpretation of the utterance. For instance, in principle, she could interpret it on the basis of (40)(a–b) and recover the proposition in (40)(c):

(40)(a)   No-one who is good at phonetics is good at semantics.
   (b)   Anyone who gives a talk on a given subject is good at that subject.
   (c)   This afternoon's speaker is not good at semantics.

However, it is unlikely that this is how the speaker intended her utterance to be interpreted. In other words, given that a hearer typically has available an enormous number of background assumptions which she could use in the interpretation of an utterance, it is essential that a theory of implicature should be able to explain how the 'correct' assumptions – that is, the ones the speaker expected to be used – are selected for use in its interpretation. How, otherwise, could it provide an account of successful communication?

1.6   The Problem of Context Selection: Mutual Knowledge Frameworks

It is clear that because of the role of the context in all aspects of utterance interpretation, a speaker who intends her utterance to be taken in a particular way must expect it to be interpreted in a context that yields that interpretation. Interpreted in any other context, a misunderstanding may arise. Thus, for example, the speaker of (37)A above will not succeed in conveying the information in (39)(b) if the hearer interprets her utterance against the assumption in (38)(a). Successful communication is achieved only if the actual context matches the one envisaged by the speaker.

In a number of accounts this has been taken to mean that for communication to be successful the context for the interpretation of an utterance must be restricted to the beliefs and assumptions shared by speaker and hearer. It might be thought that such a requirement could never be met. Not only do our different experiences of the world provide us with different beliefs about it, but also we tend to construct different representations of the same phenomena. But in fact, most of the recent discussions of the problem of context selection begin with the observation that this requirement is not strong enough.

Consider the utterance in (41) produced in response to a friend's invitation to meet her for coffee that afternoon.

(41)   There's a phonetics seminar at 3.00.

The question is whether this should be construed as an acceptance of the invitation or a refusal. Suppose the friend has guessed correctly that her friend dislikes phonetics. She cannot on this basis alone conclude that the speaker has welcomed her invitation, because the speaker might not know that her friend knows about her attitude to phonetics and might be using the seminar as an excuse for refusing the invitation. But even if the speaker knows that her friend knows about her dislike of phonetics, the friend needs to be cautious, because it is possible that the speaker might want to mislead her into thinking that she does not. And even if this possibility is covered, there is still the further and more elaborate possibility that the speaker wants to mislead the friend into thinking that she is trying to mislead her. It will be evident that, in principle, there could be infinitely many layers of deception. The only way to ensure that the interpretation recovered by the hearer is the one intended by the speaker is, it seems, to require that interpretation be based on knowledge of an infinite number of propositions. That is, the suggestion is that the context for the interpretation of an utterance must consist not just of knowledge shared by speaker and hearer, but knowledge known to be shared, and known to be known to be shared, and so on.

Knowledge of this infinitely regressive kind has been called *mutual knowledge*. It is defined more formally thus:

(42) A speaker S and a hearer H mutually know a proposition P iff:
- (i) S knows that P
- (ii) H knows that P
- (iii) S knows (ii)
- (iv) H knows (i)
- (v) S knows (iv)
- (vi) H knows (iii)

and so on *ad infinitum*.[11]

The requirement that the context for the interpretation of an utterance be restricted to full-scale mutual knowledge poses an immediate problem for a psychologically adequate account of utterance interpretation. Since a hearer has only a finite time available for interpreting an utterance, she cannot perform the infinite number of checks for establishing genuinely mutual knowledge.

Clark and Marshall (1981) argue that this problem is only apparent since there is a finite inductive procedure for identifying mutual knowledge. They claim that a speaker and a hearer can assume mutual knowledge of a proposition in virtue of their joint presence in a situation which supplies evidence for the truth of that proposition. Clark and Marshall assume that all knowledge is evidenced, and that the strength of the evidence depends on how direct it is. Accordingly, they claim that physical co-presence provides the strongest evidence for mutual knowledge, since the participants need only make minimal auxiliary assumptions in order to justify their conclusion. If, for example, speaker and hearer are sitting at a table with a dish of apples before them, they need only assume that the other is rational and paying attention in order to conclude that they have mutual knowledge of the proposition that there is a dish of apples on the table. Linguistic co-presence, they claim, provides less direct evidence for mutual knowledge: two people who are presented with the same utterance may conclude that they have mutual knowledge of the proposition it expresses only if they make a number of additional assumptions – for example, that the expressions used belong to a language they both know and that the utterance was not part of a code or some other non-standard use of language. Finally, they argue, community membership may provide evidence for mutual knowledge in the sense that if speaker and hearer can establish that they belong to the same community, then, given certain other assumptions, they can assume mutual knowledge of all the propositions known by its members.

Clark and Marshall's proposals seem to assume that all knowledge is based on the evidence of observable data. However, to acquire knowledge of a physical object or event is to derive a mental representation – a particular description – of that object or event: while the existence of a physical object might be self-evident to a sighted person, many auxiliary assumptions are required before she can establish knowledge of it under a particular description, as, for example, a dish of apples. Because these auxiliary assumptions are not necessarily themselves part of the observable data, but are supplied from memory, two different people may derive two different representations of the same object. This suggests that a speaker and hearer can guarantee that they have mutual knowledge of a proposition only if each has access to the content of each other's memory. Obviously, the fact that it is impossible for anyone to have access to anyone else's memory does not prevent successful communication from taking place.

One possible counter-argument here might be that while speakers and hearers cannot be expected to establish complete mutual knowledge, they do try to establish it to a certain degree. The question is, to what degree? Clearly, there are benefits attached to establishing as high a degree of mutual knowledge as possible. However, a psychologically adequate theory of utterance interpretation cannot ignore the costs of obtaining those benefits. How much work are speakers and hearers prepared to do in order to avoid misunderstanding?

The fact is that no matter how much work a speaker and a hearer might be prepared to do in order to establish mutual knowledge, this will not be enough to ensure that the intended interpretation of an utterance will be recovered. In interpreting the utterance in (43) the hearer aims to select a context that will supply a specific referent for the definite description *the cat*:

(43)   The cat has caught a mouse.

However, speaker and hearer might have mutual knowledge of several cats. That is, the mutual knowledge framework can only define a class of potential contexts, and cannot explain how the actual context, and hence the actual interpretation, is identified. Bach and Harnish (1979), who devote a whole book to the exposition of a particular version of the mutual-knowledge framework, recognize that they have said very little about "the specific strategy the hearer uses in identifying the speaker's actual communicative intent", and that in particular, their theory gives "no indication of how certain mutual beliefs are activated or otherwise picked out as relevant, much less how the correct identification is made" (1979: 93). But, clearly, without any such indication their theory cannot be, as they claim, a psychological description of what goes on in everyday communication (cf. 1979: 89).

Communication obviously requires co-ordination between speaker and hearer in that misunderstandings occur when there is a mismatch between the context envisaged by the speaker and the one selected by the hearer. The notion of mutual knowledge was introduced in order to provide a mechanism which, properly applied, guarantees symmetrical choices of context and, hence, successful communication. Notice that the assumption here is that failure of communication must be attributable to the improper application of communicative principles or rules rather than to the fact that these principles do not provide a fail-safe algorithm by which the hearer can identify the speaker's intentions. Moreover, it is assumed that when communication does fail the fault lies equally with speaker and hearer: both participants must take equal responsibility for establishing a sufficient degree of mutual knowledge before they proceed.

As we have seen, the fact that genuine mutual knowledge is impossible to achieve does not prevent successful communication from taking place. The successes in everyday conversation suggest that speakers do not aim to establish mutual knowledge before they proceed, but make all sorts of assumptions and guesses. These are not necessarily guesses about the assumptions or knowledge that the hearer already has available, or about the assumptions that they share. Rather, they are guesses about the hearer's ability to access certain assumptions at the appropriate moment – or, as Sperber and Wilson (1986) put it, about the hearer's *cognitive environment*. They illustrate this distinction in the following example:

Suppose Mary and Peter are looking at a landscape where she has noticed a distant church. She says to him:

(49) I've been inside that church. [Sperber and Wilson's numbering]

She does not stop to ask herself whether he has noticed the building, and whether he assumes that she has noticed, and assumes that she has noticed he has noticed, and so on, or whether he has assumed that it is a church, and assumes she assumes it is, and so on. All she has is reasonable confidence that he will be able to identify the building as a church when required to.

(1986: 43)

In fact, as Sperber and Wilson point out, it might have been only on the strength of Mary's utterance that it becomes evident to him that the building is a church: he might have thought before the utterance that it was a castle. That is, shared knowledge is a result of, rather than a prerequisite for, successful communication.

Everyday conversation is full of such examples. Consider, for instance, a situation in which A, not realizing that B is a vegetarian, has invited her to eat at the local Greek restaurant. B suspects that A does not know that she is a vegetarian. Even so, she may expect A to conclude from her response in (44) that she would prefer to eat somewhere else:

(44) All their food has meat in it.

Clearly, the information that A needs in order to derive this conclusion is not part of their shared knowledge before B made her reply. The point is that B expects that A is able to recover this information as part of her interpretation of the utterance. In other words, it is assumed not that A will have identified the intended context in advance of the utterance, but that she will construct it in the course of interpreting it.

Notice that the responsibility for avoiding misunderstanding in both these examples lies with the speaker. Mary would not have produced her utterance had she not thought that Peter was capable of spontaneously accessing the information about the church; and B would not have produced her utterance unless she thought A capable of accessing the information that B is vegetarian – that is, unless she had had some idea of A's cognitive environment. All the hearer has to do is go ahead and use what assumptions are most immediately accessible. Both participants take a risk. However, intuitively, it is clear that it is a risk worth taking: it is possible for someone who knows what assumptions a hearer is capable of making to infer which assumptions she is likely to bring to bear on the interpretation of a given utterance. The task for pragmatic theory is to describe the principles that give rise to this possibility. In the following chapter I outline an approach to utterance interpretation which is founded on the cognitive processes underlying all information processing – or, more specifically, on the notion of relevance.

2

Relevance and Communication

2.1 Grice's 'Calculability' Requirement

The principal contribution of Grice's theory of conversation (Grice 1975) was that it drew attention to those aspects of meaning that are not stipulated by linguistic (or more particularly, semantic) rules, but are worked out from the meaning of the sentence uttered together with the context on the basis of the assumption that the speaker has observed certain general principles of communication. As we saw in chapter 1, Grice called these aspects of meaning conversational implicatures, thus obscuring the fact that the context and general communicative principles play a role in the recovery of the propositional content of utterances. The distinction taken in this study to correspond with the distinction between semantics and pragmatics – that is, the distinction between linguistically determined meaning and meaning that is contextually determined in accordance with general principles of communication – is not coextensive with the distinction between what is said and what is implicated. The properties that, for Grice, characterized conversational implicatures must, on this view, characterize all aspects of meaning that fall within the domain of pragmatics.

According to Grice, the most important property of the conversational implicature of an utterance was that it should be capable of being worked out by a reasoning process, or in other words, that it should be calculable: "The presence of a conversational implicature must be capable of being worked out; for even if it can be intuitively grasped, unless the intuition is replaceable by an argument, the implicature (if present at all) will not count as a conversational implicature: it will be a conventional implicature" (1975: 50). The notion of conventional implicature will be discussed in detail in chapter 3: here it is sufficient to think of it as an example of linguistically determined meaning which falls within the domain of (linguistic) semantics rather than within that of pragmatic theory.

However, as Sperber and Wilson (1986) have pointed out, Grice's account of the derivation process is inadequate. Moreover, although a number of writers have seen the advantage of the notion of implicature for the explanation of a variety of pragmatic phenomena, there has been little attempt to make the reasoning processes involved in working out conversational implicatures explicit.

Grice proposes that the following *working out schema* is involved in the derivation of implicatures:

(1) *Working out schema for conversational implicatures*
  (a) The speaker (S) has said that p.
  (b) There is no reason to think that S is not observing the maxims.
  (c) S could not be doing this unless he thought that q.
  (d) S knows (and knows that the hearer (H) knows that he knows) that H can see that he thinks that the supposition that he thinks that q is required.
  (e) S has done nothing to stop H from thinking that q.
  (f) S intends H to think, or is at least willing to allow H to think, that q.
  (g) And so, S has implicated that q.

(1) is not recognizable as a standard logical argument. Indeed, as Wilson and Sperber (1986) point out, it is not even clear which of the steps are meant to be premises and which conclusions. They draw our attention, in particular, to the step in (c), where the content of the implicature is introduced. Clearly, this is not deducible from (a) and (b) alone: either it has to be an independent premise or it is meant to be derived from (a) and (b), together with some other unspecified premises. That is, the 'argument' seems to assume that the hearer has already identified q, the conclusion simply being that it was intended as part of the speaker's message.

However, any theory that aims to provide a method of recovering the content of the implicature must take account of another property which Grice showed to characterize implicatures, namely, that they are cancellable. Recall the example given in (20) in chapter 1 above:

(2) A: Are you coming to the talk this afternoon?
    B: It's on phonetics.

Interpreted in the context of the assumption that B never attends talks on phonetics, (2B) will convey the proposition in (3):

(3) B is not going to the talk this afternoon.

However, as we saw in the earlier discussion of this example, (2B) could have been uttered in a context in which it did not convey this proposition but, rather, the one in (4):

(4) B is going to the talk this afternoon.

Had (3) been part of the propositional content of (2B), it would have been conveyed in any context in which it was interpreted.

This point can be demonstrated further by another type of example considered in chapter 1. Conjoined utterances are often interpreted as conveying some kind of temporal or causal connection between their conjuncts. Thus, for example, the utterance in (5) might be taken to suggest that the event in the first conjunct caused the one in the second:

(5) Susan cooked a turkey for dinner and Tom fell ill.

However, it would not be contradictory for the speaker to continue her utterance by denying that there was any connection between these events. By contrast, she could not go on to deny that Tom fell ill, or that Mary cooked poultry for dinner.[1]

Levinson (1983) takes this property to be a property of the reasoning procedure by which conversational implicatures are recovered. In particular, he claims that the fact that implicatures can be cancelled in certain contexts means that they cannot be recovered by deductive (or logical) inference, but are probabilistic or recovered by inductive reasoning. The point is that whereas deductive inferences cannot be cancelled by adding further premises to the original ones, the conclusion of an inductive argument can always be invalidated by the addition of another premise. For instance, if the premises (i) and (ii) of (6) are true, then the conclusion (iii) is true, no matter what else is true or false. In contrast, the conclusion of (7) may be invalidated by the addition of the premise in (8):

(6) (i) If Socrates is a man, then he is mortal.
    (ii) Socrates is a man.
    (iii) Therefore, Socrates is mortal.
                                     (= Levinson: example (48), p. 114)
(7) (i) I have dug up 1001 carrots.
    (ii) Everyone of the 1001 carrots is orange.
    (iii) Therefore, all carrots are orange.
(8)   The 1002nd carrot is green.
                                      (= Levinson: examples (49–50), pp. 114–15)

If Levinson is right, then there is very little hope of a pragmatic theory being able to provide an explicit characterization of the reasoning procedures involved in the recovery of conversational implicatures, at least if that characterization is to consist of a set of rules for generating conclusions derived inductively from the premises. As Fodor (1983) points out, while the psychology of deductive systems has been reasonably well studied, very little is known about the psychology of inductive systems.

It will be recalled that Levinson arrived at this view of pragmatic reasoning via the distinction between context-dependent and context-independent inferences. His point was that inferences that hinge on the meanings of the words uttered, and are hence non-cancellable, are deductive, whereas cancellable inferences, which depend on the contextual information used as premises, are inductive. However, notice that the claim that pragmatic reasoning is inductive does not shed any light on the question of how the premises used in the recovery of a conversational implicature are chosen. An inductive system can only say how likely a conclusion is to be true, given the truth of the premises. That is, Levinson has not offered us anything more explicit than Grice's original working-out procedure.

In chapter 1 it was argued that the context for the interpretation of an utterance is not, as, for example, proponents of the mutual-knowledge approach would suggest, governed by a fail-safe algorithm which ensures successful communication, but a less than perfect heuristic which makes successful communication likely. According to the former approach, the cancellability of implicatures would have to be accommodated by the inclusion of an effective procedure for blocking implicatures in certain contexts. Such a procedure is provided by Gazdar (1979) for quantity or *scalar* implicature regularly recovered from sentences such as (9)(a):[2]

(9)(a) Some of the students wrote essays.
   (b) Not all of the students wrote essays.

Although (9)(a) regularly implicates (9)(b), it is possible to block its recovery, as, for example, in (9)(c):

(9)(c) Some, in fact all, of the students wrote essays.

However, it is not clear how this kind of procedure could be extended to examples such as (20) (repeated below). That is, it is difficult to see how the interpretation in (10) could be related to B's response by the application of a rule:

(20) A: Are you going to the talk this afternoon?
      B: It's on phonetics.

(10) B is going to the talk this afternoon.

Notice that all that is required for the recovery of (10) is the ability to supply the contextual assumption in (11) and use it as a premise in a logical deduction:

(11) B always goes to talks on phonetics.

However, a hearer who has access to the assumption in (11) will have access to all sorts of other assumptions any of which she could, in principle, bring to bear on the interpretation of B's response. For instance, as we saw in chapter 1, it is logically possible that she should interpret it in the context of the assumptions in (12) (a–b), thus deriving the conclusion in (12) (c):

(12)(a) Anyone who is good at phonetics is not good at semantics.
    (b) Anyone who gives a talk on a given subject is good at that subject.
    (c) The speaker of this afternoon's talk is not good at semantics.

It is this kind of logical possibility that led Levinson to conclude that pragmatic reasoning is inductive: in principle, the hearer can always bring any of her assumptions about the world to bear upon the interpretation of an utterance – just as, in principle, a scientist could use any contingently true proposition as confirmation or disconfirmation of a given hypothesis.

While this may be a logical possibility, it is not a psychological possibility. Intuitively, it is clear that the context in (12) is not one that will enable the hearer to maintain her assumption that B was producing a relevant response to A's question. That is, the hearer's choice of context (and hence her interpretation) is constrained by her assumption that the speaker is being relevant. The fact that the hearer of an utterance could in principle have brought different assumptions to bear on its interpretation does not mean that the inferences she actually makes are inductive. She performs deductive inferences from a specific set of premises. Obviously, different sets of premises may be supplied by different hearers, or by the same hearer on different occasions. However, this is simply to say that what is relevant varies from person to person and from occasion to occasion. Moreover, the hearer's search for a relevant interpretation may result in the selection of a context which does not match the one envisaged by the speaker. Successful communication cannot be guaranteed.

2.2 Deduction in a Theory of Utterance Interpretation[3]

In chapter 1 it was argued that pragmatic interpretation is a function of the so-called 'central system of thought'. That is, it involves forming a hypothesis on the basis of the input delivered from the various perceptual systems and grammar and confirming it in the light of background assumptions stored in memory. This distinction between central thought processes and input systems is due to J. A. Fodor (1983). However, as we saw, he took the scientific fixation of belief as the most typical example of the processes involved in hypothesis formation and confirmation, arguing that, because of their global nature, little can be said about them beyond that they are inferential.

As Sperber and Wilson (1986) have pointed out, Fodor's pessimism about the possibility of having a theory of the fixation of belief does not apply to utterance interpretation. Whatever we say about the computations involved in the scientific fixation of belief, pragmatic computations are subject to psychological constraints, and are consequently much more amenable to study. Their basic claim is that in processing information people generally aim to bring about the greatest improvement to their overall representation of the world at the least cost in processing. That is, they try to balance costs and rewards. Obviously, since the development of a major scientific theory will have enormous and lasting implications, it is worth spending an enormous amount of time and effort on its construction and evaluation. By contrast, in the case of such minor hypotheses as that the kettle has boiled or that it is about to rain, which are formulated spontaneously and either later abandoned or stored for future use, the costs are kept to a minimum. The fact that ordinary utterance interpretation is virtually instantaneous suggests that "however much evidence might have been taken into account, however many hypotheses might have been considered, in practice the only evidence and hypotheses considered are those that are immediately accessible" (Sperber and Wilson 1986: 66–7).

It is important to recognize, however, that the concerns of their study are not confined to linguistically conveyed information. The aim is to provide an account, not of the impact of utterances, but of the effect of information processing generally. The fact that I have just misspelt the word *psychological* will have an impact on my overall representation of the world whether I am told that I have misspelt it or I discover it for myself. This is not to say that we cannot talk of the impact – or contextual effects – of utterances. The point is that this is a derivative notion: an utterance has contextual effects only in the sense that the information it conveys has contextual effects.

Obviously, not every addition of information is an improvement: a hearer's representation of the world is not necessarily improved by the presentation of information that it already contains. Nor is it improved by the presentation of information unrelated to any of the information that it contains. The hearer's aim is to integrate new information with old, or, in other words, to recover information that is relevant to her. Notice, too, that a hearer is not just interested in obtaining more information about the world. She is also aiming to obtain better evidence for her existing beliefs and assumptions. For example, the proposition expressed by the utterance in (13) will be relevant to a hearer who, having looked at her watch, thinks that it is time for lunch:

(13) Lunch is ready.

Of course, information may also achieve relevance by disconfirming an existing assumption. Thus the hearer who had concluded from looking at her watch that it was not yet time for lunch may be led to abandon this assumption upon the presentation of the information in (13).

In this framework the hearer's overall representation of the world is taken to be the total set of propositional representations stored in memory.[4] The fact that the effect of a new item of information is a result of integrating it with existing assumptions means that the relationship between that new proposition and the context can be viewed from two different perspectives: on the one hand, it can be seen in terms of the way the context is affected, while on the other, it can be viewed in terms of the role that contextual assumptions play in assessing this effect. In this section I outline the model of the inferential abilities that Sperber and Wilson believe to be involved in the assessment of contextual effects.

A deductive inference is a formal operation which takes propositions as premises and yields propositions as conclusions. To say that an operation is formal is to say that it applies to representations in virtue of their syntactic properties rather than in virtue of their semantic content. For instance, standard logics generally include a rule of *and*-elimination which takes as premises propositions of the form $P \& Q$, and yield as conclusions propositions of the form P and of the form Q. It does not matter what the propositions taken as input are about or whether they are true: any inference of this form will be valid.

This is not to say, however, that the notion of deductive inference can be explicated without appeal to the semantic properties of the representations over which they are defined. Inferences are distinguished from other formal operations by the fact that they are truth-preserving: that is, when applied to true premises they yield true conclusions. This connection between inference and truth is usually stated as a connection between inference and entailment. Entailment is a semantic relationship which holds between two propositions *P* and *Q* if every conceivable state of affairs that makes *P* true also makes *Q* true. For example, according to this definition, (14) (a) entails (14) (b) since there is no conceivable state of affairs in which (14) (a) is true and (14) (b) false:

(14)(a) Tom is my nephew and Robert is my brother.
    (b) Tom is my nephew.

The point is that (14) (b) can be derived by the inference rule of *and*-elimination mentioned above. More generally, in a consistent logic all the propositions derived by inference rules are entailments.

From a logician's point of view, propositions are abstract objects to which abstract assignments of truth and falsity are made. The question of whether they are psychologically represented by anyone does not matter. However, here we are interested in inference rules as they apply to propositional representations stored as factual descriptions of the world – that is, to assumptions. Factual assumptions come with varying degrees of strength depending on the way they are acquired. Thus for example, assumptions derived through direct observation are generally very strong, whereas the strength of an assumption derived as a result of the interpretation of an utterance depends on the degree of confidence held in the speaker. As Sperber and Wilson point out, there are various cognitive processes involved in the acquisition of assumptions, and all of these may give rise to variations in strength. However, the process that particularly concerns us here is deduction, the point being that a conclusion inherits its strength – or, as Sperber and Wilson also call it, its confirmation value – from the strength of the premises from which it is derived.[5]

As we shall see below, inference rules are not just involved in the acquisition of new information. The fact that an inference system can be used to look for inconsistencies in the propositions submitted to it means that it can play a role in a hearer's decision to abandon an existing assumption. Further, the fact that conclusions inherit the strength of the premises from which they are derived means that inference rules can be used to assess the extent to which an existing assumption is confirmed or justified by a new item of information. In other words, from the point of view of a psychological theory of utterance interpretation, the importance of deductive inference lies in the fact that it provides an efficient means for improving a hearer's overall representation of the world by guaranteeing the accuracy of the conclusions it is used to derive.

One cannot assume, however, that any deductive system will meet the empirical standards of such a theory. In fact, there are two important respects in which the systems standardly proposed by logicians fail to meet these standards: while in the first respect standard logics are too weak (in the sense that they do not generate all the inferences we want), in the second respect they are too powerful (in the sense that they generate inferences we do not want). Let us examine these two points in turn.

In principle, standard logics aim not just at consistency, but also at completeness. That is, they aim to provide inference rules which allow us to derive every entailment as a conclusion of a valid argument. However, in practice they derive only those entailments that hinge on the presence of the so-called 'logical particles' – *and, or, if . . . then, not, all,* and *some*. For example, there are no inference rules in standard logics that derive the entailments due to the presence of connectives like *because* and *although*. The fact that (15) entails the propositions in (16) suggests the need for the rule in (17), while the entailment relation between (18) and (19) suggests the need for the rule in (20):

(15)   He left because the band started playing.
(16)(a) He left.
   (b)   The band started playing.
   (c)   His leaving was caused by the fact that the band started playing.
(17)   *Because-elimination*
         Input: P because Q
         Output: (a)   P
                   (b)   Q
                   (c)   Q is the cause of P
(18)   He left although the band started playing.
(19)(a) He left.
   (b)   The band started playing.

(20) *Although-elimination*
　　　Input:　　　P although Q
　　　Output: (a)　P
　　　　　　　 (b)　Q

Inference rules are not simply attached to the concepts represented by connectives: a complete logic would have to include the elimination rule in (23) in order to account for the fact that (21) entails (22), and the rule in (26) in order to account for the relationship between (24) and (25):

(21)　　We all know that the platypus lays eggs.
(22)　　The platypus lays eggs.
(23)　　*Know-elimination*
　　　　Input:　X know P
　　　　Output: P
(24)　　All the students are bachelors.
(25)(a)　All the students are unmarried.
　　(b)　All the students are male.
(26)　　*Bachelor-elimination rule*
　　　　Input:　[X – bachelor –Y]
　　　　Output: [X – unmarried adult male –Y]

The assumption here is that the set of words whose meanings can be explicated in logical terms is not restricted to the words like *and*, *or*, and *if . . . then*. It is generally recognized that the classical decompositionalist version of this view (cf. Katz 1972), according to which the meaning of a word is provided by a definition expressing the necessary and sufficient conditions for its application, is undermined by the existence of natural-kind terms such as *red* or *sheep*. This has been taken to mean, both by Putnam (1975) and Kripke (1975) and by proponents of 'prototype theory', that the concepts represented by such words do not have logical properties at all. However, Fodor (1981) and Fodor, Garrett, Walker, and Parkes (1980) have argued, against the decompositionalist view, that the logical properties of a concept represented by natural-kind term cannot regarded as a definition, but must instead be represented as a meaning postulate. That is, whereas *bachelor* represents a complex concept defined in terms of the logical properties captured in (26) the meaning of a word like *red* is an irreducible concept whose logical properties license certain inferences, but do not fully define it.[6] Sperber and Wilson point out that these meaning postulates can straightforwardly be represented as elimination rules. Thus, for example, the rules for *red* and *sheep* are represented in (27) and (28) respectively:

(27) *Red-elimination rule*
 Input: (X – red – Y)
 Output: (X – colour of a certain hue – Y)
(28) *Sheep-elimination rule*
 Input: (X – sheep – Y)
 Output: (X – animal of a certain species – Y)

This is not to say that the meanings of all words have logical properties. The fact that a logic does not contain inference rules associated with the range of connectives discussed in chapter 3 – for example, *therefore, after all, moreover* – should not be regarded as a shortcoming, since none of these words contributes to the truth conditions of the utterances that contain them. A complete logic need only specify those inference rules that reflect the logical properties of words whose meanings contribute to entailment relations. The point here is that there is no empirical reason for restricting our attention to the standard logical particles.

However, even if we were to restrict our attention to these particles, we should find that in order to derive all the entailments of a given set of propositions we should need rules for deriving an infinite set of conclusions from a finite set of premises. For example, the entailments of any single proposition P include those in (29):

(29)(a) not – not P
  (b) P or Q
  (c) P and P

In order to derive these entailments, standard logics provide the following rules:

(30) *Double Negation*
 Input: P
 Output: not – not P
(31) *Or-Introduction*
 Input: P
 Output: P or Q

(32) *And-Introduction*
   Input: (a) P
         (b) Q
   Output: P and Q

Sperber and Wilson note that these rules share two important properties. First, they may apply to any proposition at all regardless of its form or content; and, second, since they may apply to any proposition at all, they may apply to their own output. This means that they may apply to an arbitrary proposition P, then to the proposition derived from this first application, then to the output of the second application, and so on *ad infinitum*. Thus from an arbitrary proposition P we may obtain the following infinite sets of conclusions:

(33)(a) . . . . . not – not – not – P
   (b) ((P or Q) or R) or . . .
   (c) ((P and P) and P) and . . .

From a purely logical point of view, the existence of such rules presents no problem. However, they are not desirable from a psychological point of view. The fact that we process information in such a very short time suggests that the procedures we use must be spontaneous and finite. If these procedures involve inference, then we must either provide some means for limiting the application of these rules so that indefinite reduplication is avoided or adopt a system that does not include them.

In fact, as Sperber and Wilson point out, the problem with these rules is not just that they can be applied indefinitely, but also that the inferences they license are never drawn in the spontaneous processing of information. No hearer presented with the utterance in (34) would think that the implications in (35) were part of the speaker's intended message:

(34)   Ben rides a bicycle.
(35)(a) It's not true that Ben doesn't ride a bicycle.
   (b) Either Ben rides a bicycle or the cat has caught a mouse.

There is an intuitive sense in which these, and, indeed, any other implications derived by the use of introduction rules are trivial. This intuition can be related to the fact that introduction rules, in contrast with elimination rules, leave the content of their input propositions unchanged except for the addition of arbitrary material, or, in other words, that, unlike elimination rules, they are not genuinely interpretative. The suggestion is that the deductive system used in the processing of information includes only elimination rules and yields only non-trivial conclusions. Sperber and Wilson's definition of non-trivial logical implication is given in (36):

(36) A set of propositions $(P_1 \ldots P_n)$ *logically and non-trivially* implies a proposition Q if, when $(P_1 \ldots P_n)$ is the set of initial theses in a derivation involving only elimination rules, Q belongs to the set of final theses.

(1986: 97)

It will be noticed that all the elimination rules considered so far take only one (conjoined) proposition as input. We have ignored, for example, the rules of *modus ponendo ponens*, given in (37), and *modus tollendo ponens*, given in (38):

(37) *Modus ponendo ponens*
    Input: (a) If P then Q
             (b) P
    Output: Q
(38) *Modus tollendo ponens*
    Input: (a) P or Q   OR   (a) P or Q
             (b) not P   (b) not Q
    Output: Q   P

Sperber and Wilson call the rules which take only one proposition as input *analytic rules*, and the implications that are derived entirely by such rules *analytic implications*. Rules that take two separate positions as input are called *synthetic rules*, and any implication that is not analytic is a *synthetic implication*. In fact, to have ignored synthetic rules would have given rise to a serious lacuna in our account of utterance interpretation, for, as we shall see in section 2.3, it is these rules rather than analytic rules that are central to the deductive processing of information.

2.3 Deduction and Contextual Modification

The importance of synthetic implications in pragmatic interpretation relates to the fact that their recovery depends on having two separate propositions brought together as input to an inference rule, or, in other words, to the fact that they are not intrinsic to the content of any single member of the set of propositions from which they are derived. The analytic implications of a proposition are, by contrast, intrinsic to it: their recovery depends only on the properties of that proposition. It is this difference, suggest Sperber and Wilson, that could provide a formal basis for the pre-theoretical distinction between meaning and implication, or between explicit and implicit content. The analytic implications of a proposition, being intrinsic to its content, are necessary and sufficient for understanding its meaning: failure to grasp the analytic implications of a proposition is a failure to grasp its content. On the other hand, failure to grasp the synthetic implications of a set of propositions is not a failure to grasp the meanings of those propositions, but rather a failure to see what they imply, or, in other words, a failure to take them together as input to an inference rule.

Now, the assumptions taken as input to an inference rule may be derived from any of three sources. First, they may be delivered by the input systems, that is, by the grammar or by one of the perceptual systems; second, they may be part of the hearer's existing representation of the world, or the context; and, finally, they may be derived by deduction as analytic or synthetic implications from propositions of the first two types. As we have seen, pragmatic theory is primarily concerned with the effect of newly presented information delivered by the linguistic input system on the hearer's existing representation of the world. This means that it is concerned with a particular subclass of synthetic implications: the subclass consists of implications derived from the content of an utterance combined with premises supplied from the hearer's background beliefs. Sperber and Wilson call these implications *contextual implications*. Their definition is given in (39):

(39) *Contextual implication*
A set of assumptions {P} contextually implies an assumption Q in a context {C} iff:
(i) the union of {P} and {C} non-trivially implies Q,
(ii) {P} does not non-trivially imply Q, and
(iii) {C} does not non-trivially imply Q.

(1986: 107–8)

Recall that our aim has been to produce a definition of relevance or contextual modification that captures the following two ideas: First, establishing the relevance of a proposition is a matter of establishing a connection between it and certain accessible beliefs and assumptions; and, second, as a result of establishing this connection the hearer arrives at an improved representation of the world. It now seems that we have a basis for this definition. The recovery of a contextual implication can be regarded as adding to, and hence improving, the hearer's representation of the world, since it cannot be derived from the hearer's existing assumptions (cf. (39) (iii) above). However, a contextual implication is not just new information, since it cannot be derived from the newly presented information alone (cf. (39) (ii)). This means that a proposition P will be seen as adding to the hearer's existing representation of the world, but only as a result of its integration with certain existing assumptions. This suggests that we can define *relevance* as follows:

(40) A proposition P is relevant in a context {C} iff P has at least one contextual implication in {C}.

The intuitive appeal of this definition becomes evident when we consider the kind of response typically made by hearers who have failed to grasp the relevance of a remark – 'So what?' or perhaps just 'So?'. Such a response indicates that although the hearer has grasped the content of the utterance she cannot see what it implies, and, moreover, that she believes that she is expected to derive some implications. If she has grasped the content of the utterance, then she must have recovered its analytic implications. Her problem, then, is that she has not been able to access information that she can combine with the newly presented information for the application of a synthetic rule.

However, as has already been pointed out, newly presented information does not necessarily achieve relevance in virtue of adding to the hearer's overall representation of the world. On the one hand it may achieve relevance by providing further evidence or confirmation for existing assumptions, and on the other, it may provide evidence against, and perhaps lead to the abandonment of, existing assumptions. This suggests that the definition in (40) is too restricted.

Whereas in logic and mathematics the term *proof* is used to refer to a relationship between a conclusion and the union of the premises from which it is derived, in everyday discourse it is often extended to a relationship that holds between a synthetic implication and just one of the premises used in deriving it. Thus, for example, I could be said to present my library card as proof of my identity, even though the information on it does not by itself logically imply that I am Diane Blakemore. Similarly, to take a non-communicative example, I might regard the fact that you are reading a book on intuitionism as evidence for the fact that you have an interest in logic even though this conclusion only follows given certain other assumptions – for example, that you are understanding what you read, that you are not just carrying out a survey of the use of discourse connectives in philosophical writing, etc., etc. The fact that such conclusions are drawn, only given a context of certain other assumptions, might be taken to mean that, in contrast with the mathematical cases, the relationship is not established by the means of demonstrative inference rules, but that this is proof only in the inductive or non-demonstrative sense (cf. Levinson's arguments (1983) discussed in section 1 above). However, the only difference between the mathematical cases and the everyday ones is that whereas in mathematical proofs all the premises are made explicit, in the everyday ones some of the premises are treated as already given. Once these implicit premises have been supplied, deductive inference rules can be applied for the deduction of a conclusion in the same way that they are applied to the premises of a mathematical proof.

In fact, one could say of any case of synthetic implication that each premise implies, and hence is proof for, the conclusion only in the context of the other premises. The point is that from a purely logical point of view, there is no reason to distinguish between any of the premises taken as input to a synthetic inference rule: the only thing that matters is that they are all jointly necessary for the derivation of the conclusion. From a cognitive point of view, however, the decision to draw attention to the relationship that holds between the conclusion obtained, Q, and just one of the premises used in obtaining it, P, is not arbitrary, but it arises out of the nature of the interest served in establishing it. Recall that we are interested in the processes by which a hearer recovers information which improves her existing representation of the world. As we have seen, information from that existing representation is taken as input to these processes. But the point is that old information, by definition, cannot itself count as an improvement, but only as the context in which the implications of new information are assessed. Hence the definition of a particular subtype of synthetic implication defined in terms of a relationship between P and Q in a context $\{C\}$.

Notice that the discussion that led to this definition ignored the fact that assumptions come with varying degrees of strength. Since deductive rules contribute not only to the formation of new assumptions, but also to the determination of their strength, we must ask how the relative strength of the premises is related to the strength of the conclusion obtained. Suppose, for example, that I see you taking a pile of books out of the library, all with Russian titles. As I have mentioned earlier, assumptions derived from direct observation tend to be very strong. That is, it is likely that I am certain of the truth of the assumption in (41):

(41) You are taking some Russian books out of the library.

However, intuitively, it is clear that I am not entitled to be as certain of the conclusion I draw from this assumption, given in (42):

(42) You know Russian.

The point is, of course, that (42) is not logically implied by (41) alone: it follows only given the assumptions in (43):

(43)(a) Anyone who takes books out of the library intends to read them.
    (b) One can read a book only if one knows the language in which it is written.
    (c) One can only intend to do what one can do.

Whereas premise (43) (c) is certain, premises (43) (a) and (b) are less than certain. This variation in the strength of the premises affects the strength of the conclusion so that it can only be as great as the strength of the weakest premise. Hence the intuition that the assumption in (42) is less than certain even though it was contextually implied by an assumption whose certainty I did not doubt. More generally, an assumption obtained by deduction can only be as strong as the weakest premise used.

Let us assume now that some days after the library incident I see you at a screening of a Russian film without subtitles. On the basis of this observation together with the assumptions in (44) I again draw the conclusion in (42):

(44)(a) One could not understand this film unless one knew the Russian language.
   (b) You understand this film.

Once again, I do not hold all these assumptions with equal certainty: while I may be certain of (44) (a), I may not be certain of (44) (b) – you could always be pretending to understand it. This would suggest that, again, the conclusion in (42) is less than certain. However, intuitively, it is clear that my assumption that you know Russian is stronger now than it was after the library incident. Previously, I had only one piece of evidence for it. Surely, the fact that I now have two independent pieces of evidence must strengthen my conviction. More formally, when a conclusion C is derived independently from two sets of premises, $\{P\}$ and $\{Q\}$, then it should inherit a degree of strength from the union of $\{P\}$ and $\{Q\}$ which is greater than the one it inherits from $\{P\}$ and $\{Q\}$ independently.[7]

The effect – which Sperber and Wilson call *independent strengthening* – is achieved when two sets of premises yield the same conclusion. Let us now see what happens when two sets of premises yield contradictory conclusions. Suppose, for example, that after the library incident, instead of seeing you at a Russian film I had met you at a party where, during a discussion about foreign languages, you produced the utterance in (45):

(45) I wish I knew Russian.

This utterance conveys the proposition in (46), which, of course, contradicts the assumption in (42):

(46) You do not know Russian.

Clearly, I cannot hold both (42) and (46). How am I to resolve the contradiction?

Intuitively, the answer is clear: I must abandon one of them.

That is, one assumption must be erased from my memory. Moreover, in the situation described, it is clear which of the two assumptions I am likely to retain – the one in (46). The point here is that in producing the utterance in (45) you give a guarantee that the proposition in (46) is true. Given that I have no reason to doubt you, I shall regard (46) as more likely to be true than (42). Accordingly, I shall abandon (42) in favour of (46). In other words, when it is possible to compare the relative strength of two contradictory assumptions, it is possible to resolve the contradiction by abandoning the one for which there is less support.

In this section we have seen that there are three ways in which a newly presented proposition may have a contextual effect: it may lead to the formation of a new assumption; it may strengthen an existing assumption; or it may lead to the abandoning of an existing assumption. In each case the hearer is left with a modified set of background assumptions which are available for use in assessing the effect of the next proposition, which itself contributes to the background for the interpretation of the next, and so on. In other words, a hearer does not simply aim to identify the proposition with which she has been presented: she also aims to work out the consequences of adding it to a set of propositions which have already been processed. Indeed, there seems to be little point in a hearer's being able to identify a proposition unless she can see its consequences for what she assumes already. By the same token, there seems to be little point in someone offering a hearer information unless she has ground for thinking it will have some effect on her existing assumptions. For example, although it is probable that you can identify the proposition expressed by (47), it is unlikely that you will be able to see the point of my utterance, given the assumptions that you have in mind at the moment:

(47)   I work in Southampton.

It is not enough for you to recover an item of information you didn't have before: you must be able to relate it to assumptions you have already. That is, your aim is to establish its relevance.

However, notice that while it is unlikely that you can relate the proposition expressed by (47) to the contextual assumptions at the forefront of your attention, it is unlikely that you cannot access some context in which it has some impact. For example, on the basis of the assumption in (48)(a), you will be able to derive the contextual implication in (48)(b):

(48)(a) Southampton is in the south of England.
   (b) The author works in the south of England.

In other words, (47) is not totally irrelevant: it is simply less relevant than many other propositions that I could have presented here – for example, the proposition in (49):

(49)   I have almost finished this section.

Clearly, it is not enough to say that the hearer's aim in interpreting an utterance is to recover a proposition that has some relevance. For since, in principle, any of the assumptions accessible in her cognitive environment could be brought to bear in establishing the relevance of a proposition, this would mean that her interpretation is not constrained at all. Nor is it sufficient to say that the speaker's aim in producing an utterance is to present information which is relevant, for this would mean that she could produce just any utterance. The suggestion is that it is not just relevance, but optimal relevance that should form the basis of our pragmatic theory. In the next section I shall show how this notion, together with certain very general properties of communication, lead to the formulation of a principle which, according to Sperber and Wilson, underlies all communicative behaviour.

2.4   The Principle of Relevance

Intuitively, it is clear that other things being equal, the greater the contextual effects of a newly presented item of information, the greater its relevance for the person processing it. Thus, for example, in normal circumstances the fact that the light goes on in my study when I turn the switch has less implications for me, and hence less relevance, than the fact that it does not go on. However, it has to be remembered that all information-processing requires effort and time – that is, a cost – and that, other things being equal, the greater the cost of processing a new item of information, the less its relevance for the person processing it. In the case of verbally communicated information there are two types of costs involved. On the one hand, there are the costs entailed by the linguistic complexity of the utterance: the more complex the utterance the greater the processing effort required. On the other, there is the cost of accessing and using contextual assumptions. Since the main thesis of this study hinges on an understanding of the psychological constraints on context selection, it might be as well to consider this last point in more detail.

In the earlier discussion of inference and its role in information-processing it was emphasized that inference rules are purely formal operations applying to propositional representations in virtue of their form or structure. However, little was said about the structure of propositional representations. In particular, nothing was said about the components or constituents of their structure. Sperber and Wilson have proposed that a proposition can be treated as a structured string of concepts, a concept being a label or, more technically, an address for various types of information: (a) logical information; (b) lexical information; and (c) encyclopedic information. The general idea is that when a concept appears in a proposition being processed, access is given to the various types of information stored under that heading.

The logical entry for a concept consists of the set of inference rules that apply to propositions of which that concept is a constituent. For example, the logical entry for *and* will include the rule of *and*-elimination mentioned earlier. The encyclopedic entry for a concept contains information about the extension or denotation of the concept – that is, about the objects, properties, or events that instantiate it. For instance, the encyclopedic entry for *Southampton* in the proposition expressed in (48) might include the information in (50):

(50)   Southampton is in the south of England.
       Southampton is a port.

Finally, the lexical entry for a concept contains information about the natural-language word or phrase that expresses it.

This classification raises a number of important questions. In the first place, although the distinction between logical and lexical entries seems clear cut, there is a question about how much of the overall interpretation process should be handled in linguistic terms (that is, by lexical entries) and how much in logical terms.[8] Second, the distinction between logical and encyclopedic entries might be interpreted as suggesting that there are two fundamentally different kinds of truth – truths of 'meaning' (traditionally called 'analytic truths') and truths of fact (traditionally called 'synthetic truths'). This distinction is notoriously contentious.[9] However, Sperber and Wilson point out that the distinction between logical and encyclopedic entries is based not on the claim that there is a difference between two kinds of truth, but rather on the claim that information must be representable in two different forms and function in two different ways if successful communication is to take place – that is, on the distinction between computations and the representation over which those computations are performed. The information in the logical entry is computational: it consists of a set of inference rules that apply to propositions in which the concept appears. In contrast, the information in the encyclopedic entry is representational: it consists of a set of propositions to which inference rules may be applied. The claim that encyclopedic entries are representational is fundamental to the inferential account of information processing being outlined here. For, according to this account, if the context for the interpretation of a proposition is determined by the encyclopedic entries of the concept it contains, then those entries must contain information that can supply the input to a synthetic inference rule. That is, if inference rules are involved in information-processing, so must propositions be: neither notion can exist without the other. This is not to say that information that is represented computationally at one time could not be represented propositionally at another, or that information represented computationally by one person could not be represented propositionally by another. The point is that both inference rules and propositional representations are needed for a theory of information-processing, and that the distinction between them is reflected in the distinction between logical and encyclopedic entries.

It is generally agreed that encyclopedic information in long-term memory is organized into units or packages. This idea, which has its origins in Artificial Intelligence and has been described in various ways – for example, in terms of *frames* (Minsky 1975), *schemas* (Rumelhart and Norman 1978), and *scripts* (Schank and Abelson 1977) – has been adopted by a number of writers interested in the interpretation of discourse. Thus, for example, van Dijk (1977) appeals to the notion of a frame in order to account for what he calls the 'macro-structure' of texts – that is, the way in which individual sentences are integrated into a text. Samet and Schank (1984) account for textual coherence in terms of the notion of a script – or, in other words, a network of conceptual dependencies.[10]

Sperber and Wilson also assume that encyclopedic entries are *chunks* which themselves may be grouped into larger chunks, and contain smaller chunks. However, as we shall see in the final chapter of this study, their approach to the role of the context in utterance interpretation is fundamentally different from the coherence-based approaches just mentioned.[11]

Sperber and Wilson's aim is to provide a principle that constrains the interpretation of all discourse, whether it consists of a sequence of utterances or of a single utterance. On their view, understanding an utterance is a matter of integrating the proposition it expresses with a context of existing beliefs and assumptions. As we shall see, the contextual assumptions used in interpretation of an utterance may have been made available by the preceding discourse – indeed as Blass (1985) has shown, this is what characterizes a coherent text. However, equally they may be derived from a non-communicative event.

In the coherence-based approaches the fact that the textual appropriateness of an utterance cannot be established independently of the context is taken to mean that the notion of a sentence grammar must be widened so that we can talk of a grammar of discourse or a text grammar. For example, van Dijk (1977) suggests that in order to account for the well formedness of discourse we need to include in our grammar a pragmatic component with rules relating sentence-context pairs to interpretations at a global level of semantic description (macrostructure). The problem is that in principle a text can give the hearer access to a number of knowledge packages (frames), not all of which are actually used. For example, van Dijk proposes that for the interpretation of the sequence in (51) the hearer accesses a frame containing knowledge of a stereotypical economic phenomenon:

(51) In the past it [the town of Fairview] had been a go-ahead prosperous little town, and its two large factories, specialising

in hand-tools, had been a lucrative source of wealth.
(1977: 132)

However, it is not clear from his account why the hearer is not expected to access a 'town frame' or a 'tools frame'. Furthermore, not all information in a frame will be used in the interpretation of an utterance. If there are rules for determining whether a given utterance is an appropriate continuation of a discourse, then there must be rules for selecting the contextual information used in establishing the required relationships.

For Sperber and Wilson, utterance interpretation is not a matter of encoding and decoding messages according to rules. Nor is it a matter of bringing any arbitrary subset of assumptions to bear as a context. The actual context for the interpretation of an utterance is constrained by "the organisation of the individual's encyclopaedic memory, and the mental activity in which he is engaged" (1986: 138).

Although, typically, a hearer will have an enormous amount of encyclopedic information available to her in memory, only a small subpart of this will be accessible to her at any given moment. Moreover, not all information will be equally accessible to her at any given time. For example, the most easily accessed will include the information that has been recently processed – for example, the information that played a role in the interpretation of the immediately preceding utterance, together with the information derived from it. Sperber and Wilson propose that this information is part of an initial or immediately given context which can be extended in various ways. For instance, in the case of verbal communication a hearer may extend the initial context to include not only the interpretation of the immediately preceding utterance, but also the interpretation of utterances occurring earlier in the discourse. Alternatively, the interpretation of an utterance may lead the hearer to extend her initial context by adding information derived from her physical environment. Recall Sperber and Wilson's example in which Mary, looking at a distant building, produces the utterance in (52):

(52) I've been inside that church.

It is quite possible that until Mary spoke, her audience had not even noticed the building to which she has referred. However, it is likely that he will be able to re-assess his environment, notice the building, and add it to his memory under the description of a church.

Finally, notice that the concepts present in the initial context or in the proposition being processed will themselves give the hearer access to encyclopedic entries which in turn contain concepts which are addresses for further entries, and so on. That is, it is possible for a hearer to extend her context via the concepts contained in the assumptions she is currently processing. For example, the utterance in (48) (repeated below) may give the hearer access to the encyclopedic entry for *Southampton*, which, assuming that it includes the assumption in (53), may in turn give her access to the encyclopedic entry for *port*, which, if it includes the assumption in (54), will give her access to the encyclopedic entry for dockworker:

(48)   I work in Southampton.
(53)   Southampton is a port.
(54)   Ports employ dockworkers.

In principle, the hearer could go on adding to her context indefinitely. Does this mean that the context for the interpretation of an utterance is of an indefinite size?

Notice that each extension of the context involves a cost: that is, the cost of accessing the entry for *dockworker* is greater than that of accessing the one for *port*, which is in turn more costly to access than the entry for *Southampton*. Furthermore, as the size of the context increases, so does the cost of using the assumptions that it contains in the interpretation of an utterance. And as these costs increase, other things being equal, the relevance of the new information will decrease. The basic claim underlying Sperber and Wilson's theory is that in processing information individuals automatically aim to achieve the best possible balance of effort and time against the contextual effects gained – or, in other words, that they automatically process each new item of information in the context in which it yields a maximum contextual effect for the minimum cost in processing. This means that a hearer who is searching for relevance will extend the context only if the costs this entails seem more likely to be offset by contextual effects.

This claim is a claim about all information-processing. That is, the goal of maximal relevance governs the way in which people process all incoming information, whatever its source. However, Sperber and Wilson point out that there is a substantial difference between the way in which people approach information that has been intentionally communicated and the way they approach information from other sources. Obviously, a person will pay attention to a phenomenon only if she thinks that it will be worth her while – that is, only if she thinks that by doing so she will be rewarded by some improvement to her overall representation of the world. For someone processing information not intentionally communicated there is no guarantee that her efforts will be rewarded at all. In other words, she may only have hopes of a satisfactory degree of relevance. In contrast, a person who has been deliberately presented with information can have not just hopes that her efforts will be rewarded, but expectations. In other words, an act of communication brings with it a guarantee that there is information worth processing.

This guarantee derives from a very general fact about human interaction. If you attract my attention, for example, by waving, or speaking, to me, then you suggest that you believe that you have information that is relevant to me and hence worth processing. Otherwise there would be no point in your attracting my attention in the first place. So if you deliberately attract my attention, and if I recognize that you are deliberately attracting my attention, then I shall expect that I shall be able to recover some relevant information.

As we have seen, a hearer is not just interested in obtaining some reward: her aim is to achieve the greatest contextual effect for the available processing effort. This means that it is in her interests that the information presented to her is the most relevant information available to the communicator. However, a communicator will have her own aims, and these may lead her to give the hearer information whose impact is less than that of other information she could have given. Nevertheless, to be worth the hearer's attention it must have some impact.

We have also seen that accessing contextual assumptions and using them to derive contextual effects involves a cost, and that the cost of deriving contextual effects in a small, easily accessible context will be less than the cost of obtaining them in a larger, less accessible context. This means that it is in the interests of a hearer who is aiming for relevance that the communicator should produce an utterance whose interpretation calls for less effort than any other utterance she could have made to achieve the same effects. There are always a number of ways of conveying the same information, and while these all may involve the same amount of effort from the communicator's point of view, their interpretation may require varying amounts of effort from the hearer. Consider, for example, the discourse sequences in (54) and (55) (both taken from Blass 1985):

(55)   He went into MacDonalds. The quarter pounder sounded good and he ordered it.
(56)   The river had been dry for a long time. Everyone attended the funeral.

Blass assumes that whereas the first sequence would present little difficulty for a Westerner, the second will seem incomprehensible. That is, whereas the mention of *MacDonalds* gives the hearer access to an encyclopedic entry which can be brought to bear on the interpretation of the next, in (56) there is nothing in the interpretation of the first utterance that could give access to contextual information that could be used in the interpretation of the second. In contrast, for a speaker of Sissala the sequence in (55) would yield no contextual effect, whereas the one in (56) would be perfectly comprehensible.

A Western speaker who wished to communicate the information in (55) to a Sissala hearer would have to make the required contextual assumptions explicit – that is, by producing the sequence in (57) – while a Sissala speaker who wished to communicate the information in (56) would have to produce the sequence in (58):

(57)   He went to a place where food is cooked and sold. It is called MacDonalds. There he saw ground meat which was formed into patties, fried, and put into something baked with flour . . .
(58)   If a river has been dry for a long time, then a river spirit has died. If someone has died, then there is a funeral. The river had been dry for a long time . . .

Obviously, these sequences are much more complex than the corresponding sequences in (55) and (56). However, the complexity is the price the speaker must pay to ensure successful communication. That is, they provide the most relevant means for communicating the information in question. In contrast, the sequence in (57) would be far less relevant to a Westerner than the one in (55): the extra effort spent in processing it would not be offset by an increase in contextual effects. Similarly, someone from the Sissala culture would find (58) much less relevant than (56).

The point is, of course, that no speaker who wished to communicate with a Western hearer would have produced the sequence in (57). Given that she does want to communicate, it is in her interests to make her utterance as easily understood as possible. Indeed, any Western hearer presented with (57) might doubt that genuine communication was intended, and might even refuse to make the processing effort required. In other words, the presumption of relevance carried by every act of deliberate communication has two aspects: on the one hand it carries a presumption of adequate effect, while on the other, it carries a presumption of minimally necessary effort. Taken together, these presumptions define a level of optimal relevance. Sperber and Wilson call the principle that gives rise to the presumption of optimal relevance the *Principle of Relevance*.

On the view adopted in this study, the need for a pragmatic theory arises from the fact that the linguistic properties of an utterance seriously under-determine its interpretation: it will include referential expressions with undetermined referents; it may contain ambiguous or vague expressions; it may be elliptical; and its intended illocutionary force may not be fully determined. Moreover, there are aspects of interpretation for which no linguistic clue is given at all. Thus, for example, there is no linguistic rule linking B's response in (59) (repeated below) and the assumption in (60):

(59) A: Are you going to the seminar this afternoon?
B: It's on phonetics.
(60) B is not going to the seminar this afternoon.

Sperber and Wilson's claim is that the Principle of Relevance is sufficient to explain the role of contextual assumptions in all these aspects of interpretation. Briefly, the hearer's task is to recover the interepretation that is consistent with her presumption that the information conveyed will yield adequate contextual effects in return for the minimum necessary processing. As we have seen, the hearer is entitled to this presumption simply in virtue of recognizing that an act of communication had taken place. Of course, the guarantee of relevance may be based on mistaken, or even fraudulent, grounds: the speaker may always be mistaken about the hearer's ability to supply the requisite contextual assumptions, or she may be attempting to mislead the hearer about the relevance of the information she is offering. However, the point is that any act of communication comes with the communicator's guarantee of relevance, and as long as the hearer has confidence in this guarantee, she will simply go ahead and recover the interpretation that is consistent with it.

2.5 Implicature

On this view the responsibility for success in communication is not shared, but taken solely by the speaker. On the assumption that the speaker has aimed at optimal relevance, the hearer will simply go ahead and recover the optimally relevant interpretation. This means that a speaker who wants communication to succeed must have grounds for thinking that the hearer has immediate access to a context in which contextual effects can be obtained, and, indeed, the very fact that she has spoken shows that she believes that she does have such grounds.

But are the contextual effects that the hearer obtains those intended by the speaker? The conception of interpretation and communication underlying this question is one that has dominated recent pragmatic theory: it is generally assumed that in communicating the speaker has a specific communicative intention which the hearer must identify if communication is to be successful. Within this framework the sole concern of pragmatic theory is the explanation of how the hearer recovers not just any interpretation, but the one the speaker intended. The processes by which hearers recover unintended information are excluded on the grounds that they are undertaken on the hearer's initiative and constrained by her own interests rather than by her desire to identify the speaker's intentions. In other words, on this view pragmatic interpretation necessarily involves a certain amount of speaker–hearer co-ordination.

Notice, however, that not all communication involves the recovery of contextual effects specifically intended by the speaker. If, for example, a stranger approaches you in the street and asks you the time, then you may assume that your answer is relevant to her without having any particular idea of the contextual assumptions that she will bring to bear on its interpretation. You will simply assume that the hearer has access to some context in which the information you are offering her is relevant.

In other cases the speaker may have an idea of the range of contextual effects her utterance will have, but not have any specific expectations about the conclusions the hearer will draw. Consider, for example, how the utterance in (61) might be interpreted if made by one friend to another in a shop where piped music is being played:

(61) I can't stand this type of music.

Although this utterance is clearly intended to have some contextual effect, it is rather difficult to pin down. There is a wide range of contextual assumptions that the hearer could supply, and hence a wide range of contextual effects she could obtain: the hearer is simply expected to recover an interpretation that falls somewhere within this range.

Obviously, speakers do have more specific expectations about the way in which their utterances will be interpreted. Moreover, hearers do interpret utterances in the way they are expected to. Thus, for example, if you and I had previously agreed that we would listen to a radio programme which starts at five past seven, it would be reasonable for me to expect you to interpret my utterance in (62) as conveying one of a fairly narrow range of propositions such as the one in (63):

(62) It's seven o'clock.
(63) The programme starts in five minutes.

Within the mutual-knowledge framework (discussed in chapter 1) this example would be taken as a demonstration of the way in which successful communication depends on speaker–hearer co-ordination on the choice of context. Our agreement provides a basis for mutual knowledge which, when brought to bear on the interpretation of my utterance, yields the intended interpretation. The processes involved in deriving this interpretation are, according to this view, totally different from the processes involved in the recovery of any other suggestions.

Our agreement certainly does give me grounds for thinking that you will be able to access the contextual assumptions required for the interpretation of my utterance. However, this is not to say that prior to my utterance I stopped to check that you knew that we were going to listen to the programme, and that you knew I knew that we were going to listen to it, and so on. For all I knew, you could have completely forgotten about it. The point is that I had reasonable confidence that you would be able to access the required information upon hearing my utterance. Indeed, there would have been little point in my producing the utterance at all had I thought otherwise.

Given that I did produce the utterance, you have a guarantee that you will be able to obtain adequate contextual effects in return for the minimum cost in processing. This means that you are justified in assuming that any information you recover as a result of processing my utterance in the smallest and most accessible context possible is the ground on which I based my guarantee. In other words, the Principle of Relevance licenses you to assume that the least costly interpretation is the one I intended. This is not to say, of course, that I could not be mistaken about your ability to supply the required contextual premises. Communication can fail. Nor is it to say that you may not bring to bear other contextual assumptions to derive other contextual effects. The point is that the success of any extra processing you undertake cannot be guaranteed under the Principle of Relevance.

In this example it is clear that although the speaker had fairly specific expectations about the way in which her utterance would be interpreted, the hearer was free to choose whatever contextual assumptions yielded adequate contextual effects for a minimum cost in processing. The point was that the speaker had grounds for thinking that the hearer would recover the intended interpretation of her own accord. There was no need for her to make it clear that she did expect this interpretation to be recovered. That is, there was no need to constrain the hearer's interpretation in any way.

Now let us consider a different example. Suppose that Tom offers Susan an apple which has a small sticker on it saying 'Cape'. Tom does not know what this sticker means – that is, that the apple was exported from South Africa – and Susan suspects that he doesn't know this. Nevertheless Susan may expect Tom to interpret her response in (64) as conveying the information in (65):

(64)   I never eat South African fruit.
(65)   Susan does not want to eat the apple.

This example bears a resemblance to the one discussed at the end of chapter 1 in which A, not realizing that B is a vegetarian, asks her to eat at a Greek restaurant, and receives the reply in (66):

(66)   All their food has meat in it.

The point there was that the hearer was able to recover the intended interpretation (that is, the proposition that B would prefer to eat somewhere else) even though the contextual assumptions required were not mutually known by A and B prior to the utterance, or, in other words, that mutual knowledge is not a prerequisite for successful communication. Similarly, the information that Tom needs to recover the information in (65) was not part of Susan's and Tom's shared knowledge before Susan made her reply in (64). In fact, Tom will come to have this knowledge as a result of interpreting the utterance.

Obviously, Susan would not have made this response unless she thought that Tom could access the required contextual assumptions – that is, unless she had grounds for thinking that he could access the assumption in (67):

(67)   The apple comes from South Africa.

However, it is evident that Susan is not really taking a risk here. Indeed, it is difficult to see how Tom could have interpreted the utterance in any other way. Let us see why.

By asking Susan whether she would like the apple, Tom is suggesting that he has immediately accessible a context in which either the information that she does want it or the information that she doesn't is relevant. This means that Susan would have satisfied the Principle of Relevance by answering him directly. But (64) is not a direct answer to Tom's question. If Tom wishes to maintain his assumption that Susan was aiming at optimal relevance, he will have to assume that she expects him to supply the contextual premise in (67) and then to deduce the answer in (65). Notice that Susan may expect Tom to supply this premise not because she has grounds for thinking that it is already highly accessible to him, but rather because her utterance made it accessible to him. In other words, by answering him indirectly she has constrained his choice of context and directed him towards a particular interpretation.

At this point it might be objected that there is an indefinite number of contexts that could be used in the interpretation of (64), and that there is no logical reason why Tom mightn't have been expected to derive the same answer by supplying completely different contextual assumptions, or, indeed, why he mightn't have been expected to derive a different answer altogether. There is, for example, no logical reason why he might not have supplied the contextual premises in (68) and then have deduced the proposition in (69):

(68)(a) People who don't eat South African fruit are left wing.
    (b) Left wing people eat healthy food.
    (c) Apples are a healthy food.
(69)   Susan wants to eat the apple.

However, while there may be no logical reason for recovering one interpretation rather than another, there is a psychological reason. Recall that according to the account outlined in section 2.4, hearers interpret utterances on the assumption that the speaker has aimed at optimal relevance. This means that hearers may be expected to interpret each utterance in the smallest and most accessible context that yields adequate contextual effects. Whereas Susan's reply, together with Tom's question, gives Tom immediate access to the context in (67), they only give indirect access to the context in (68). Each expansion of the context requires effort. Moreover, given that the context in (68) is larger than the one in (67), it can be assumed that the costs of using it to derive contextual effects are greater. In other words, although (68) does yield contextual effects, their recovery would be too costly in processing terms. No speaker aiming at optimal relevance would produce an utterance like (64) in the context of Tom's offer expecting it to be processed in a context like (68).

The claim that hearers interpret utterances on the assumption that the speaker has aimed at optimal relevance might be taken to suggest that utterance interpretation involves listing all the possible interpretations and then ranking them according to their degree of relevance. However, this strategy is inconsistent with the Principle of Relevance. As Sperber and Wilson say, "if the only way of finding the right interpretation were to list and rank all possible interpretations, then all possible interpretations would require the same amount of effort; namely the effort needed to construct and compare them" [1986: 166]. The point is that given his assumption about the accessibility of the context in (67), a speaker aiming at optimal relevance would not expect the hearer of (64) even to consider the possibility in (68). For according to the Principle of Relevance a hearer could not be expected to spend effort either in extending this context or in investigating other lines of processing when the original hypothesis already yields adequate contextual effects. In other words, the only interpretation warranted by the Principle of Relevance is the first one found to be consistent with it.

But why should a speaker who is aiming at optimal relevance have produced the utterance in (64) in the first place? In producing an indirect answer Susan has forced Tom to access the context in (67) and to deduce (65) as a contextual implication. Each of these steps requires processing effort which would not have been required for the interpretation of the direct answer. How can we reconcile these extra steps with the assumption that the speaker was trying to minimize processing effort?

Once again, we need to recall that according to the Principle of Relevance, a hearer may expect that any time and effort he spends will have some reward, and hence that any additional processing costs will be offset by an increase in contextual effects. This suggests that Tom can maintain his assumption that Susan was aiming at optimal relevance if he assumes that she believes that the information she has offered is more relevant than the direct answer – that is, if he assumes that she believes it will yield contextual effects not derivable from the direct answer. For example, it may be that Susan wants to alert Tom to the significance of the label on the apple so that he does not make the same offer again, or perhaps, assuming that Tom shares her opinion about buying

South African produce, so that he will avoid buying fruit with these labels. Or perhaps Susan simply wants Tom to know that she is a person with principles. Notice that it may not be clear to Susan exactly what extra effects Tom will recover. The point is simply that Susan must believe that it is worth while for Tom to undertake the extra processing entailed by her indirect answer.

Grice (1975) used the term *conversational implicature* to refer to any proposition derived by the hearer from an utterance as a consequence of her assumption that it conforms to the Maxims of Conversation (see 1.5 above). It is generally accepted that the main value of this notion is that it captures the way in which speakers can convey more than what they actually say – or, in other words, the way in which utterances have implicit import as well as explicit content. Unfortunately, as we have seen, his account of the processes by which such propositions are derived are not adequate. However, Sperber and Wilson have now provided a framework in which the implicit import of utterances is derived by inferential processes constrained by a single, psychological principle. In this framework we can distinguish between two categories of implicit import. On the one hand, there are the assumptions that the hearer recovers as conclusions of the deduction – that is, the implicated conclusions – while on the other, there are the contextual assumptions that the hearer supplies as premises in order to derive these conclusions. Thus, for example, the proposition in (65) is an implicated conclusion, and the one in (67) is an implicated premise.

The examples discussed in this section range from one in which the speaker had no expectations at all about the way his utterance would be interpreted to ones in which the speaker constrained the hearer's choice of context so that a specific interpretation was recovered. In between, we have examples like (61) in which there was a whole range of conclusions the hearer could have drawn, and ones like (62) in which the hearer was expected to recover a conclusion from a much narrower range. Pragmatists have generally ignored the first type of case completely on the grounds that it does not involve identification of the speaker's intentions. However, we have seen that the processes involved are of the same nature (that is, inferential) and constrained by the same principle (the Principle of Relevance) as the ones in examples like (64). This is not to say that there is no difference between these examples at all. For while we definitely do want to talk about the implicit import of Susan's utterance in (64), we would not want to say that your response to the stranger's request for the time has implicit import. There is nothing you wanted to convey beyond the explicit propositional content of the utterance.

In contrast, there is something specific Susan wanted to convey in addition to the explicit propositional content of (64) – that is, the conclusion in (65). Or to put the same point differently, there was a specific context she had in mind – the assumption in (67). In fact, as we have seen, the hearer was given no alternative but to access this premise and derive this conclusion. However, in forcing Tom to undertake this processing Susan expected him to derive a range of further contextual effects. Clearly, since Susan expected Tom to derive these effects, we do want to say that they are part of the implicit import of her utterance. Yet they are implicated in a rather different way from the propositions in (65) and (67).

This property of indeterminacy of implicit import, which is also exhibited by (61) and (62), was noticed by Grice:

> Since to calculate a conversational implicature is to calculate what has to be supposed in order to preserve the supposition that the Co-operative Principle has been observed, and since there may be various possible specific explanations, a list of which may be open, the conversational implicatum in such cases will be a disjunction of such specific expectations; and if the list of these is open, the implicatum will have just the kind of indeterminacy that many actual implicata do in fact seem to possess.
>
> (1975: 58)

Such indeterminacy is difficult to reconcile with Grice's earlier suggestion that a conversational implicature is a proposition specifically intended by the speaker. In view of examples like (69) and (60) it would seem preferable to adopt Sperber and Wilson's use of the term *implicature* to refer to the whole range of contextual assumptions and implications from which the speaker expects the hearer to select in interpreting her utterance in accordance with the Principle of Relevance.

As we have seen, such indeterminacy is a matter of degree. Sperber and Wilson suggest that given the varying degrees of indeterminacy, we might distinguish strong from weak implicatures. The strongest possible type of implicated assumption is one selected from a set containing only one member. Implicated assumptions that are selected from a small range of alternatives are strong, but not as strong as when there are no alternatives. Implicated assumptions selected from a wide range of alternatives are relatively weak, and become weaker as the range of alternatives increases.

In all these cases the hearer's interpretation is constrained by the Principle of Relevance. However, notice that in the case of (62) the hearer was under a much tighter constraint than the hearer of, say, (60). There was only one way in which she could interpret the utterance in order to see it as consistent with the Principle of Relevance. In other words, the effect of the indirect answer was to constrain the hearer's interpretation by making a specific contextual assumption immediately accessible, thus ensuring correct context selection at minimal processing cost. This constraint is a purely pragmatic (that is, non-linguistic) one: imposing it is a matter of exploiting the presumption of relevance. In chapter 3 I shall consider a number of ways in which the speaker may use the form of her utterance in order to constrain the hearer's choice of context under the Principle of Relevance – or, as Grice might have put it, the use of conventional means for specifying implicit import.

3

Linguistic Form and Pragmatic Interpretation

3.1 Conventional Implicature

Grice's theory of conversation (Grice 1975) is generally associated with an attempt to maintain an approach to semantics according to which the meanings of all linguistic expressions can be analysed in terms of their contribution to the truth conditions of the utterances that contain them. Indeed, the idea that there are aspects of utterance interpretation that are determined by general pragmatic principles has often led to the conflation of linguistic semantics and propositional (or truth-conditional) semantics so that, on the one hand, it is assumed that linguistic meaning cannot determine non-truth-conditional aspects of utterance interpretation, while on the other, it is assumed that pragmatic principles cannot play a role in determining the propositional content of utterances.

We have already seen that the second of these assumptions cannot be maintained. Wilson and Sperber (1981) have demonstrated that pragmatic principles play a part in disambiguation, reference assignment, the resolution of vagueness, and the recovery of ellipsed or unexpressed material. We shall be looking at some more recent proposals about the role of pragmatic principles in the recovery of propositional content in chapter 4. Here, however, my main concern is with the first assumption – that is, the assumption that all linguistic meaning can be defined truth-conditionally. It will be recalled that Grice himself questioned this view when he introduced the notion of conventional implicature. His (tantalizingly brief) comments concerned the use of *therefore* in (1):

(1)   He is an Englishman; he is, therefore, brave.

According to Grice's analysis, this use of *therefore* indicates that his being brave is a consequence of his being an Englishman. However, the speaker could not have been accused of speaking falsely should the consequence in question fail to hold.

Karttunen (1974) and Karttunen and Peters (1975) link this notion to the class of phenomena referred to in the presupposition literature as 'pragmatic presuppositions' (cf. Stalnaker 1974, 1975). They recognize that the latter term has been used to cover a heterogeneous class of phenomena, and hence that it is unlikely that everything that has been called a pragmatic presupposition is in fact a case of conventional implicature. Nevertheless they claim that what Grice says about *therefore* in (1) applies equally well to sentences with such words as *manage, fail, again, even, yet*, and *too*, all of which have been said to carry pragmatic presuppositions.[1]

Unfortunately, all that Grice actually said about *therefore* was that its meaning does not contribute to truth conditions. He did not go on to say what it did contribute to. Certainly, this property is shared by the lexical items Karttunen and Peters mention. Thus, for example, the speaker of (2) suggests that it wasn't easy for John to find a job, and that his finding a job must have taken some effort:

(2) John managed to find a job.

However, the speaker would not have said anything false were this not to be the case. The truth of (2) depends solely on the truth of the proposition in (3):[2]

(3) John found a job.

Karttunen (1974) points out that some words interact with intonation for their non-truth-conditional effect. For example, according to the way it is pronounced, the sentence in (4) can implicate any of the propositions in (5):

(4)   My car starts badly too.
(5)(a) Someone else's – you know whose – car starts badly.
   (b) Something else of mine – you know what – starts badly.
   (c) My car does something else – you know what – badly.

However, all the various pronunciations express the same proposition, namely, that my car starts badly. *Too* makes no contribution to truth conditions.

Karttunen also points out that conventional implicatures are not always attributable to the meaning of individual words, and that they may be associated with certain grammatical constructions. For instance, whereas the use of the cleft construction in (6) suggests that the proposition in (8)(a) is being taken for granted, the use of the construction in (7) suggests that the proposition in (8)(b) is being taken for granted:

(6)   It was Ben who ate the apple.
(7)   It was the apple Ben ate.
(8)(a) Someone ate the apple.
   (b) Ben ate something.

However, this not a difference of truth conditions: both utterances are true if and only if Ben ate the apple.

We shall be considering focus-related phenomena in more detail later in this chapter. In the meantime I wish simply to make some general remarks about Karttunen's (and Karttunen and Peters') approach to all these non-truth-conditional phenomena – lexical and non-lexical.

Since Karttunen accepts the existence of linguistically specified non-truth-conditional elements of meaning, he cannot identify linguistic meaning with truth conditions (or with what he calls 'logical form'): "Words like *too* have no place in logical form" (1974: 12). However, he does assume that the truth-conditional (or semantic) aspect of the meaning of an utterance is fully determined by its linguistic properties – an assumption which we have seen cannot be maintained:

> Let us assume that the truth conditional aspect of the meaning of a natural language sentence is captured by mapping each syntactic derivation of the sentence onto a corresponding logical form. . . . The logical form of the sentence together with the meaning postulates for the language in question determine what proposition the sentence expresses, that is, what class of worlds the sentence corresponds to.
>
> (1974: 1–2)

Basically, for him there is only one distinction that matters: the distinction between the semantic (that is, the truth-conditional) and the pragmatic (that is, the non-truth-conditional). The role of pragmatic principles (general Gricean principles governing the use of language) is restricted to the non-truth-conditional, but linguistic meaning straddles both the truth-conditional and the non-truth-conditional – or, in other words, the semantic and the pragmatic.

The fact that linguistic meaning can play both a truth-conditional role and a non-truth-conditional one is the central concern of this study. However, I do not share Karttunen's view that truth-conditional meaning is determined exclusively by linguistic meaning. Moreover, as I hope to show in this chapter, a proper understanding of the non-truth-conditional role of linguistic meaning hinges on an appreciation of the distinction between the roles of linguistic knowledge and of non-linguistic knowledge in utterance interpretation, or, more particularly, on the understanding of the general psychological constraints on the use of non-linguistic information.

The need for a proper account of context in a theory of conventional implicature is, in fact, implicit in Karttunen's own suggestion about the role of words such as *too* in the interpretation of the utterances that contain them. *Too*, he says, is a "rhetorical device" whose presence or absence does not have any bearing on what proposition the sentence containing it expresses, but rather relates the sentence "to a particular kind of conversational context" (1974: 12). In other words, such expressions impose constraints on the context in which the utterances containing them must be interpreted. If the appropriate context is not available, then the utterance (that is, the use of the word in question) is inappropriate or infelicitous. Karttunen owes much of this idea to Stalnaker's (1974) proposals about the relationship between pragmatic presuppositions and 'common ground'. The basic claim is that at each point in a conversation there is a set of propositions that all participants are rationally justified in taking for granted, either by virtue of what has been said in the conversation, what they are in a position to perceive as true, or by virtue of whatever else they mutually know or assume. In the course of the conversation these presumptions may change. However, it cannot be changed by uttering just any sentence. For a sentence may conventionally implicate a proposition that is not already part of the common ground, and in this event conversation would be disrupted.

We have seen that the identification of the context for the interpretation of an utterance with the knowledge or beliefs shared by the speaker and hearer cannot be justified. Conversation is not always disrupted when a speaker produces an utterance whose interpretation requires the hearer to supply contextual assumptions that were not already part of her overall representation of the world. Indeed, in many cases the hearer comes to have these contextual assumptions only as a result of interpreting the utterance. Nevertheless it does seem to be the case that by producing an utterance of a particular form a speaker may give a guarantee not just that the information she is offering is relevant, but that it is relevant in a specific context – or, in other words, that it is relevant in a particular way. Moreover, a speaker who indicates that she expects her utterance to be interpreted against a particular set of background assumptions signals her commitment to their truth. This means that if, as in the example given by Karttunen and Peters, a speaker indicates that the following discourse is to be interpreted as relevant against a set of contextual assumptions whose truth is controversial, conversation will be disrupted. Each of the two most relevant responses to (9) would signal the acceptance of the proposition in (10):

(9) Did you forget to ring Harry?
(10) I (the hearer of (9)) intended to ring Harry.

As Karttunen and Peters say, in order to disassociate herself from (10) the hearer must digress from answering the question.

The proposal, then, is that conventional implicatures should be analysed as linguistically specified constraints on contexts. But why should there be such devices? And how do we reconcile their existence with the claim outlined in chapter 2 that all utterance interpretation is constrained by a single general principle? In fact, it is this general principle that provides an explanation for the notion of conventional implicature. Recall that according to the Principle of Relevance the hearer is entitled to interpret every utterance in the smallest and most accessible context that manifestly yields adequate contextual effects. This means that if the speaker wishes to constrain the interpretation that the hearer recovers, then she must constrain her choice of context by making the necessary assumptions immediately accessible, thus ensuring their selection at minimal processing cost. That is, she must direct the hearer to a particular set of assumptions.

Given this, the cases of implicature considered in the final section of chapter 2 might seem rather paradoxical. For there is a sense in which in producing an indirect answer, a speaker constrains the hearer's interpretation by increasing her processing costs. For instance, the indirect answer given by Tom in (11) entails more processing than the direct one would have. Yet Tom may exploit the hearer's assumption that his reply is consistent with the Principle of Relevance in order to convey the information in (12):

(11) Ben: is Susan rich?
 Tom: ALL lawyers are rich.
(12) Susan is rich.

In order to preserve her assumption that Tom was aiming at optimal relevance the hearer must supply the contextual premise in (13):

(13) Susan is a lawyer.

The fact that Tom has forced the hearer to access this assumption and to derive (12) as a contextual implication may be explained if the extra processing effort these steps require is offset by the recovery of contextual implications that would not have been derivable from the direct answer. In other words, the extra information he gives must have some relevance of its own.

In contrast, since conventional implicatures do not contribute to the propositional content of the utterances that contain them, their use could not be said to add any extra information. Their sole function is to guide the interpretation process by specifying certain properties of context and contextual effects. In a relevance-based framework, where the aim is to minimize processing costs, the use of such expressions is to be expected.

In this chapter I shall show how this approach can be applied to a number of non-truth-conditional phenomena, including some of the ones discussed by Karttunen. However, for the most part I shall be pursuing the line of enquiry suggested by Grice's example in (1), by considering the role of those expressions that are used to express inferential connections between propositions in discourse.

3.2 Premises and Conclusions: Evidence and Justification

As we have seen, Grice suggested that the use of *therefore* in (1) (repeated below) indicates that the fact of his being brave is a consequence of his being an Englishman:

(1) He is an Englishman; he is, therefore, brave.

The problem with this account is that the term *consequence* can refer either to a causal effect or to a logical conclusion. Did Grice mean that *therefore* indicates that his bravery was caused by his being an Englishman, or did he mean that it indicates that the fact that he is an Englishman is evidence for the belief that he is brave? In other words, does *therefore* indicate a causal relation between states of affairs or an inferential relation between propositions?

The distinction I have in mind here is reflected in the ambiguity of utterances containing the subordinating conjunction *because*. In (14) the clause introduced by *because* can be interpreted either as stating the cause of Tom's departure or as providing evidence for the belief that Tom has left:

(14) Tom has left because his wife isn't here.

Notice that it is only in the former interpretation that the meaning of *because* contributes towards the truth conditions of the utterance. In the second (non-causal) interpretation the speaker could have spoken truly even if the fact in the first clause is not proven by the fact in the second. Moreover, it is only in this first interpretation that *because* can fall under the scope of logical operators such as negation. For example, (15) can be interpreted either as stating the cause of Tom's failure to leave or as denying that the absence of Tom's wife caused his departure – that is, either as (16) or (17). However, when the *because* is interpreted as introducing the evidence for a belief (15) can only receive the reading in (18):

(15) Tom hasn't left because his wife isn't here.
(16) It is because Tom's wife isn't here that he (Tom) hasn't left.
(17) It isn't because Tom's wife isn't here that he (Tom) left.
(18) It is because his wife isn't here that I believe that Tom hasn't left.

It will be recognized that when a *because*-clause introduces evidence for the belief expressed in the first clause, the two clauses are generally separated by tone-group boundary. That is, the *because*-clause is bracketed off intonationally. The suggestion is that this tone-group boundary serves as an intonational clue as to the scope of logical operators.[3]

Returning now to Grice's example in (1), it will be noticed that *therefore* is bracketed off intonationally from the rest of the utterance – that is, it is parenthetical. Given this, we should not expect to find it falling under the scope of sentential operators. And, indeed, Kempson's (1975) argument that Grice's non-truth-conditional analysis of *therefore* is mistaken does not appeal to the parenthetical use of *therefore* exemplified in (1), but involves the use of *therefore* in a co-ordinate structure where it can receive focal stress. Thus she argues (p. 214) that in (19) the suggestion that Mary's bruises were caused by Bill's hitting her can be embedded within the scope of the conditional so that the truth value of the sentence depends on whether the connection actually holds:

(19) If Bill hit Mary and therefore she was covered in bruises, she will have won her suit for damages.

Kempson claims that if it is true that Bill hit Mary and that Mary was covered in bruises, but false that Mary's bruises were caused by Bill's hitting her, then even if it is false that Mary won her suit for damages, (19) will be true.

It is difficult to assess this argument. As it stands, it rests on the (rather dubious) assumption that the natural-language connective *if . . . then* has the meaning of the material-implication sign in formal logic. It seems that Kempson should have made the different, and much stronger, point that if the two conjuncts of the antecedent are true, but the causal connection expressed by *therefore* does not hold, then even if it is true that Mary won her suit for damages, (19) will be false.

No matter how we interpret the conditional, it is clear that Kempson takes *therefore* to be expressing a causal connection between two states of affairs (Bill's hitting Mary and her being covered in bruises), and not a deductive connection between two propositions (cf. Kempson 1975: 145). In other words, she takes it to mean 'as a result of that' or 'because of that'. On this interpretation, it seems, *therefore* can contribute to the truth conditions of the utterance that contains it. However, equally, in this use it must be distinguished from Grice's (parenthetical) *therefore*. This suggests that we could accommodate Kempson's example by saying that *therefore* is ambiguous between a truth-conditional causal sense and a non-truth-conditional inferential sense.

At this point it might be observed that everything I have said about *therefore* could be said about *so*. Like *therefore*, *so* expresses a relation of consequence, and can be embedded within the scope of logical operators when used in a conjoined utterance. However, even if we do allow a causal sense of *so* in addition to its purely inferential sense – a possibility which will be questioned in section 3.3 – there are cases in which *so* is evidently not expressing a relation of causal consequence and yet still falls under the scope of a logical operator. I shall postpone the discussion of these cases until chapter 4, when we examine the interpretation of conjoined utterances in more detail. Meanwhile I shall simply note that the possibility of *so* and *therefore* falling under the scope of logical operators arises only when they are used in a conjoined utterance, a use which, as we shall see, cannot be analysed in terms of the way in which these words constrain the relevance of the proposition they introduce.

Let us, then, restrict our attention to the non-conjoined cases such as the one discussed by Grice. The point is that, as it is used in Grice's example, *therefore* expresses not a causal connection, but an inferential one. (1) does not mean (20). Nor does (21) mean (22).[4]

(20) He is an Englishman. Because of that he is brave.
(21) Tom's wife is not here. Therefore he has left.
(22) Tom's wife is not here. Because of that he has left.

This conclusion receives additional support from the fact that *therefore* is not always used to introduce a proposition that is a factual description of the world:

(23) She's your teacher. Therefore, respect her.
(24) She's your teacher. Therefore, you must respect her.

In (23) the first proposition is being asserted not as evidence for a belief, but as a reason for carrying out a command. In (24) *therefore* does not preface a command; however, the modal auxiliary can be given a deontic interpretation in which it signals that the speaker is recommending that the hearer respect her. In both cases, then, *therefore* is being used where the speaker wishes to provide evidence for the desirability of a certain state of affairs. This suggests that deduction may play a role in assessing the extent to which a new item of information affects the strength of a non-factual assumption.[5] However, the point here is that in neither example could *therefore* be construed as expressing a causal connection between the states of affairs represented by the propositions expressed.

Notice that the question we are discussing here, of whether *therefore* expresses a relation of logical consequence or of causal effect, simply does not arise in the case of *after all*, as it is used in the following:

(25) He is brave. He is, after all, an Englishman.
(26) Tom has left. After all, his wife is not here.

The proposition introduced by *after all* can only be interpreted as providing evidence for the truth of the first proposition. That is, (26) would never receive the interpretation in (27):

(27) It is because Tom's wife is not here that he has left.

It will, of course, be recognized that although both *therefore* and *after all* are used to express a logical or deductive relationship, they are not used to express the same logical relationship: whereas *therefore* introduces a conclusion (the consequence), *after all* introduces a premise (the evidence). In other words, *after all* expresses the same logical relation as *because* in the use discussed above. However, this is not the only difference between *therefore* and *after all*. *After all* is not simply used to indicate that the proposition it introduces is meant to be interpreted as evidence for the proposition in the previous clause. In contrast with *because*, it also suggests that the speaker has grounds for thinking that the proposition it introduces is already accessible to the hearer.

How can a proposition that is already contained in the hearer's belief set be relevant? Notice that although the information that Tom's wife is not here may be contained in some part of the hearer's memory, it may not necessarily be contained in the most immediately accessible context. In particular, it may not be contained in the context made accessible by the speaker's use of *after all* – that is, the context in which the logical relation between the two propositions in the sequence can be established. But this is the context in which the proposition that Tom's wife is not here is relevant: the hearer has been instructed to establish its relevance by establishing the connection. In general, a hearer who is presented with a proposition which is neither contained in, nor logically implied by, the most immediately accessible (or initial) context, but is contained in some larger accessible context, will understand the utterance as a reminder. A reminder is relevant only in the contexts that do not contain the information it expresses.[6] However, as we have seen, the proposition introduced by *after all* in (26) is more than a reminder – or, at least it is a very special type of reminder. For the hearer is given a specific instruction as to the way in which it is to be interpreted as relevant.

It will be recognized that the smallest context in which the proposition introduced by *after all* in (26) can be interpreted as a premise for the deduction of the proposition in the first clause is the one in (28):

(28)   If Tom's wife is not here, then he (Tom) has left.

Similarly, it will be recognized that in order to establish the connection expressed by *therefore* in Grice's example in (1), the hearer will supply the additional contextual premise in (29):

(29)   All Englishmen are brave.

Indeed, in all the cases mentioned so far it is impossible for the hearer to establish the required connection unless he supplies further premises from the context.

Now, it will be recalled that inference rules are either analytic, taking only one proposition as input, or synthetic, taking more than one proposition as input. On the basis of the observation just made, we might want to say that in general *therefore* is used to introduce a proposition that is derived as output to a synthetic inference rule, and that *after all* is used to introduce a proposition that is part of the input to a synthetic inference rule. However, there seems to be a subtle difference in the extent to which this generalization holds. For instance, it seems that the use of *therefore* in (30) is more acceptable than the use of *after all* in (31):

(30) Tom is a bachelor. Therefore he's not married.
(31) Tom is not married. After all he's a bachelor.

Admittedly, the utterance in (30) is the sort of utterance one would only make in classes in semantics or logic. Nevertheless, it is difficult to imagine a (serious) speaker producing (31) in these situations.

The explanation of this discrepancy follows from the point made earlier: a speaker's use of *after all* indicates that she has grounds for thinking that although the proposition it introduces is contained in some part of the hearer's accessible memory, it is not contained in, or implied by, the initial context. But in this case the initial context – that is, the propositions most recently processed – does imply the proposition in question, which means that it cannot be interpreted as relevant in the specified context.

At this point, it may be objected that *after all* can in fact be used to introduce a proposition which is a premise in an analytic inference. Consider, for example, the utterance in (32):

(32) You can't divide 997 by anything other than itself. After all it's a prime number.

The idea here is that once you have the concept of a prime number, you have its logical entry and hence the proposition in the first clause. However, recall that the distinction between logical and encyclopedic entries is based not on the claim that there is a fundamental difference between two types of truth, but rather on the claim that information must be representable in two different forms if successful communication is to take place. According to this view, information represented at one time in the logical entry for a concept could at some other time be represented propositionally. This means that a proposition that is an analytic implication from a purely logical point of view could in practice be derived by the application of a synthetic inference rule. Given this view, one might speculate that the difference between (31) and (32) is due to the fact that a hearer is more likely to represent the logical entry for prime number propositionally than she is the logical entry for *bachelor*.

But surely we need to explain not just why (31) is odd, but also why (30) is not odd. How could a speaker who presents the conclusion to an analytic inference, having just presented the premise, be aiming at optimal relevance? The point here is that while it may be the case that Tom's being not married logically implies his being a bachelor, it is not necessarily the case that the hearer will know this is the conclusion she is meant to draw on this occasion. There are all sorts of conclusions she might have derived, including the analytic implication that Tom is male. This suggests that, in contrast with *after all*, the effect of *therefore* is to constrain the relevance of the proposition in the preceding clause (by indicating that it is relevant as a premise for the deduction of the proposition *therefore* introduces).

It remains to explain, then, how a proposition marked as a premise in an inference is relevant. What is the purpose of getting the hearer to establish an inferential connection between two propositions? In section 3.1 we saw that a logical-deduction system provides hearers with a means for automatically computing the effects of adding a new proposition to an existing set of assumptions. In particular, we saw that an inference system is not just used for deriving new information which is added to the hearer's existing representation of the world, but also for establishing the extent to which new information provides further evidence for an existing assumption. The point was that assumptions about the world come with varying degrees of strength, and that logical computations assign strength to conclusions on the basis of the strength of the premises from which they are derived. Thus if the hearer has immediate access to a context in which a newly presented proposition licenses the deduction of the proposition that has just been processed, then she would have grounds for thinking that it was offered as evidence or proof. Equally, a hearer who has immediate access to a context in which a newly presented proposition licenses the deduction of a proposition which the speaker subsequently presents will have grounds for thinking it is relevant as evidence for that second proposition. Notice that the extent to which a hearer regards a proposition as proven will, in both cases, depend not just on the strength of the premise actually offered, but also on the strength of any additional premises supplied from the context. For, as we have seen, the strength of a conclusion can only be as great as the strength of the weakest premise. This means, for example, that while the hearer of (1) might accept the hearer's word that he is an Englishman, she might not accept this as conclusive proof that he is brave: it all depends on the degree to which

Linguistic Form and Pragmatic Interpretation

she accepts the proposition in (29) as a factual description of the world.

The suggestion, then, is that a speaker indicates that the hearer is expected to establish an inferential connection between two propositions for the purpose of showing that the proposition marked as premise is relevant as evidence or justification for the other. However, as we shall see in the following section, this is not the only purpose that may be served by this inferential connection.

3.3 Premises and Conclusions: Implication and Explanation

The discussion so far has been restricted to examples in which a word expresses an inferential connection between two propositions presented by a single speaker. There is, of course, no reason why two speakers may not share responsibility for presenting an argument or proof so that one presents a premise and the other the conclusion. However, in such cases the second speaker will be understood to be continuing the first speaker's utterance rather than responding to it. In contrast, consider now the dialogue in (33):

(33) A: You take the first turning on the left.
B: So I don't go past the hospital.

Although B's use of *so* indicates that the proposition it introduces is a conclusion derived from the proposition expressed by A's utterance, neither speaker will be understood to be participating in the presentation of an argument or proof. Rather B's utterance is relevant as confirmation of (or as a request for confirmation of) the relevance of A's utterance. That is, she is confirming that the proposition her utterance expresses is indeed a contextual implication of A's utterance.

Sometimes, of course, a hearer may not be able to see the relevance of a remark at all. The typical response in such cases is simply 'So?' or 'so what?', but not, I believe, 'Therefore?'. The relative unacceptability of *therefore* in such situations may be attributable to stylistic considerations rather than to a difference in meaning between *so* and *therefore*. Nevertheless, the fact remains that a speaker's use of a word that indicates that the proposition it introduces is a conclusion is not always associated with proof or justification. In some cases, as in (33), it may be used in the course of checking the relevance of a remark. In others, for example (34), it may be used to draw attention to an implication of a previous utterance.

(34) A: Tom's car isn't here.
B: So he decided not to come after all.

There are all sorts of reasons for drawing the hearer's attention to a specific contextual implication of a remark. It may be that the speaker has grounds for thinking that the hearer does not have the contextual resources to derive the implication on her own initiative. Or it may be that the speaker believes that the hearer has derived the implication, but has not attached sufficient importance to it. Whatever the reason, however, it is clear that a speaker will only draw attention to a particular implication if she believes that this will itself yield some contextual effect. In (34) the use of sentence-final *after all* (which is to be distinguished from the *after all* discussed in section 3.2) indicates what this effect is. Thus B may be taken to be drawing attention to the implication of the absence of Tom's car for some previous conversation in which the likelihood of Tom's presence has been discussed.

It is not necessarily the case, of course, that a speaker may only draw attention to, or confirm, the effect of another speaker's remark. In (35), for instance, the speaker may be understood to be musing on the implications of her first remark:

(35) There's $5 in my wallet. So I didn't spend all the money then.

Nor is it the case that a speaker may only draw attention to the implications of a proposition that has been deliberately communicated. For example, a speaker who has just seen someone arrive home laden with parcels might produce the utterance in (36):

(36) So you've spent all your money.

Clearly, *so* is not being used here to indicate that the proposition it introduces is proven by what has just been said. More generally, a proposition may provide proof only if it itself comes with a guarantee of factuality, and, as we have seen, only communicated propositions come with any sort of guarantee of relevance. Here, then, the speaker is simply drawing attention to a proposition which she has derived from her observation of a given state of affairs or event.

This is not to say that the use of *so* is never associated with proof. Thus in (37) *so* might be regarded as a more informal means of conveying the inferential connection expressed by *therefore*:

(37) This suggestion can be cancelled without contradiction. So it is an implicature.

On the other hand, the fact that *so* may be used either in the course of an argument or in the course of specifying the relevance of some previous utterance does not necessarily mean that it is ambiguous between a justificatory meaning and a non-justificatory one. Its meaning in both uses is the same: an instruction to interpret the proposition it introduces as a logical consequence. The fact that this instruction may serve either a justificatory or a non-justificatory purpose follows from the fact that a logical deduction system may be used either for establishing the extent to which newly presented information provides evidence for an existing assumption or for deriving new information which is added to the hearer's existing representation of the world. The purpose served by the inferential connection expressed by *so* on a given occasion will be determined by the context and the Principle of Relevance.

At this point it might be objected that if *so* is not ambiguous between a justificatory and a non-justificatory sense, it is ambiguous between an inferential and a non-inferential or causal sense.[7] That is, it may be claimed that although in the examples already discussed *so* introduces a logical consequence, in examples such as (38) and (39) it introduces a causal effect.

(38) Tom ate the condemned meat. So he fell ill.
(39) I was bored. So I left.

One may attempt to accommodate such examples by conflating the notions of causal effect and deductive consequence so that relationships perceived to hold between states of affairs are explained in the same terms as relationships established between representations of states of affairs. However, this seems to undermine the very distinction that allows us to talk of propositions as representations of the external world. On the other hand, saying that *so* has a causal meaning in addition to the inferential meaning just discussed seems to be contrary to the Gricean spirit of the pragmatic framework I have adopted in this study.

If *so* does express a causal connection, then we should be able to substitute it for expressions like *because of that* or *as a result* without change of meaning or acceptability. However, it seems that there are utterances where the substitution of *so* for these expressions yields an unacceptable or different result. Compare, for example, the sequence in (40) with the one in (41):

(40) Tom ate the condemned meat. Because of that/As a result he fell ill thirteen hours later.
(41) Tom ate the condemned meat. So he fell ill thirteen hours later.

Whereas (41) would be acceptable only to a hearer who assumed that anyone who ate the condemned meat would fall ill thirteen hours later, the acceptability of (40) does not depend on such a context. This suggests that whereas expressions like *as a result* are used to assert a causal connection, the use of *so* assumes it, or, in other words, that whereas the causal connection is part of the propositional content of (40), in (41) it is a contextual assumption that the hearer is expected to supply in order to establish the inferential connection expressed by *so*. More generally, it seems that the causal flavour of utterances like (38) and (39) is due to the fact that the inferential connection the hearer is expected to establish depends on a contextual premise expressing a generalization about a causal link between events of the type represented in the first proposition and those of the type represented in the second.

Causal connections also figure in explanations. Thus, for example, the proposition introduced by the expression *you see* in (42) is an explanation for the event described in the first proposition, only given the assumption that there is a causal connection between ice and slipping:

(42) She slipped. You see, the road was icy.

Linguistic Form and Pragmatic Interpretation

Clearly, not all explanations appeal to such causal connections. One would not want to say, for example, that the speaker of (43) is assuming a causal connection between Mondays and going out:

(43) She's not here. You see, it's Monday.

Rather, the hearer is expected to supply an assumption such as the one in (44):

(44) She goes out every Monday.

Notice that this assumption together with the proposition introduced by *you see* licenses the deduction of the first proposition of the sequence. The suggestion, then, is that a proposition introduced by *you see* is relevant as an explanation for an event/state of affairs in virtue of the fact that it is a premise for the deduction of the proposition describing that event/state of affairs. It will be recognized that in this respect *you see* plays a role identical to that played by (sentence-initial) *after all*. Both expressions introduce a premise. However, whereas the premise introduced by *after all* is suggested to be an assumption already held by the hearer, *you see* introduces entirely 'new' information. As we saw in section 3.2, a proposition already assumed by the hearer may be relevant as a reminder. In the case of utterances with *after all* the speaker reminds the hearer of an assumption in order to justify a proposition she has just presented, or, in other words to raise its factuality. In contrast, a speaker uses *you see* to indicate that the proposition it introduces is relevant as an explanation for the proposition she has just presented. There is no suggestion that the hearer does not believe this proposition or does not believe it with sufficient certainty. The presentation of this proposition has simply raised the question 'Why?' or perhaps 'How?'.

The point here is that if I come upon an event, for example the event of someone slipping, then it is possible that I can see other things that enable me to derive the reason for its occurrence. I may, on the other hand, need to be told, in which case the presentation of the second proposition of the sequence of (43) will be relevant as an answer 'Why did she slip?' If I am simply told that someone slipped, then it is much less likely that I shall be able to supply the explanation for myself and the speaker will have stronger grounds for presenting me with it. That is, she will have good reason for thinking that the second proposition of (43) is relevant as an answer to a question raised by the presentation of the first.

According to this account, it is the presentation of the first proposition of a sequence like (43) that provides the speaker with grounds for thinking that the second proposition is relevant. The need for an explanation is created by the presentation of the first proposition. Similarly, one might say that the relevance of a proposition introduced by *after all* is created by the presentation of the preceding proposition. In this case the speaker presents the proposition only because she has already presented a proposition which requires justification. Obviously, the need to provide either explanation or justification may not be anticipated in advance, and in this respect utterances prefaced by *you see* and *after all* may be regarded as afterthoughts or repairs.

It might be thought that the same point could be made about utterances involving *so*. And, indeed, in some cases it seems that a speaker will present a proposition as a conclusion simply in order to specify the relevance of a previously presented proposition, or, in other words, simply to meet the need created by the hearer's apparent inability to establish the relevance of the previous remark. Since this need may not be anticipated in advance, utterances prefaced by *so* may also be regarded as afterthoughts. More importantly, in such cases the fact that the speaker has presented a proposition Q in a sequence P. *So* Q need not indicate anything more than a belief that the hearer wants a specification of the relevance of P.

In other cases, however, the fact that a speaker has drawn attention to a particular contextual implication of an earlier remark is evidence for her belief that this contextual implication has its own relevance – that is, relevance over and above the fact that it is a contextual implication of a proposition that has just been expressed. In these cases, the sequence P. *So* Q is to be taken as an indication of the speaker's belief that both the original proposition (P) and its implication (Q) are relevant to the hearer and that the hearer is not expected to derive Q from P on her own initiative. It is difficult to see how this may not be anticipated in advance, and hence, in these cases, utterances prefaced by *so* cannot be thought of as afterthoughts.

Linguistic Form and Pragmatic Interpretation

In chapter 4 I shall show that the distinction that is emerging here may help to account for the fact that *so*, but not *after all* or *you see*, may express an inferential connection within a conjoined utterance. However, before we consider the interpretation of conjoined utterances let us continue with our survey of inferential connections in discourse by turning to the analysis of *moreover*, *furthermore*, and *also*.

3.4 Additional Premises

In this section we shall consider the role of an expression which, although it does not connect propositions as input and output to an inference rule, must nevertheless be analysed in terms of logical consequence. In (45) the proposition in the second sentence is neither derived from the proposition in the first sentence nor a premise for the deduction of the proposition:

(45)   He is an Englishman; he is, moreover, brave.

Nevertheless, it is evident that these propositions must be understood as being connected through inference and that the fact they must be understood in this way is due to the meaning of *moreover*. More specifically, *moreover* indicates that these propositions are related as premises.

Now, to say that two propositions, P and Q, are connected as premises is to say that they are premises for the same conclusion, C. However, this is compatible with two different types of relationship: First, one could be saying that P and Q are combined as premises in the same argument. In this case, the effect of *moreover* is to indicate that C cannot be obtained from P alone. Alternatively, one could be saying that P and Q are premises in different arguments, both of which have C as conclusion, in which case the effect of *moreover* is to indicate that there is a conclusion which can be derived from P which can also be derived from Q. Whereas in the first case P and Q are jointly necessary for the deduction of C, in the second case Q will be understood as additional support for a proposition which is assumed to have been derived from P.

In fact, it seems that *moreover* can be used in both cases. Consider first (46):

(46) Susan has bought a tracksuit. Moreover, she had a salad for lunch.

If we assume that the second proposition in (46) is being presented as additional evidence or support for whatever the first proposition is evidence for, then we must assume that the hearer is expected to construct an argument of the form (47)(a) and then construct an argument of the form (47)(b):

(47)(a)   P   (47)(b)   Q
            . . .   additional   . . .
            . . .   premises   . . .
            ─────   ─────
              C   C

Now, there are all sorts of conclusions that the hearer might have derived from the first proposition of (46) (that is, *P*) which she could not have been expected to derive from the second proposition (i.e. *Q*). For example, the hearer might have accessed the contextual assumption in (48)(a) and derived the conclusion (48)(b):

(48)(a) If Susan has bought a tracksuit, she probably intends to go jogging.
  (b)   Susan probably intends to go jogging.

Clearly, no speaker aiming at optimal relevance could have expected the hearer to derive (48)(b) from the second proposition of (46).

This suggests that *moreover* indicates that the hearer is expected either to process the first proposition in a different context or to process it further. In either case the context that she accesses for the first proposition and the context she accesses for the second proposition must yield the same conclusion. The hearer could meet this requirement by accessing (49)(a) for the interpretation of the first proposition and (49)(b) for the interpretation of the second:

(49)(a) If Susan has bought a tracksuit, then she intends to lose weight.

(b) If Susan ate salad for lunch, then she intends to lose weight.

Combined with the first proposition of (46), (49)(a) yields the conclusion in (49)(c):

(49)(c) Susan intends to lose weight.

But this conclusion is also obtained when (49)(b) is combined with the second proposition of (46). In this way *moreover* constrains the hearer's choice of context not only for the interpretation of the proposition it introduces, but also for the interpretation of the proposition in the preceding sentence.

What is the point of providing the premise for an argument whose conclusion can be obtained from a proposition which has already been presented? Recall that in processing information a hearer aims to acquire not just more beliefs about the world, but also better-evidenced beliefs. As we saw in chapter 2, logical deduction plays a central role in assessing the extent to which a newly presented proposition confirms an existing assumption by virtue of the fact that a proposition derived in an inference inherits its strength from the premises used to derive it. When a conclusion is derived from two separate sets of premises $\{P\}$ and $\{Q\}$, then it will inherit a degree of strength from the union of $\{P\}$ and $\{Q\}$ greater than the one it inherits from either $\{P\}$ or $\{Q\}$ alone. In other words, by presenting a proposition that is a premise for the deduction of a conclusion that she had already conveyed, the speaker is able to increase the strength of her guarantee of its factuality.

Let us now consider an utterance which consists of just the first sentence of (46). (We shall call this utterance (46)(a)):

(46)(a) Susan has bought a tracksuit.

While the speaker of (46)(a) can be regarded as having guaranteed the factuality of the proposition that she has expressed, she has not guaranteed the factuality of any proposition that the hearer might derive from it, for example, the proposition in (48)(b) or even (49)(c). In Sperber and Wilson's terminology this proposition is either recovered entirely on the hearer's initiative or only weakly implicated. However, in uttering the second sentence of (46) (repeated below as (46)(b)), the speaker indicates explicitly that she is offering the proposition it expresses as evidence for the factuality of some proposition *C* and hence that she is offering a guarantee of the factuality of *C*:

(46)(b) Moreover, she had salad for lunch.

As we have seen, this proposition *C* must be one that can be derived from the proposition in the preceding sentence (that is, from (46)(a)). But this means that the effect of (46)(b) is to constrain the interpretation of (46)(a) so that it must be interpreted as evidence for *C*. Thus, whether the hearer had derived (49)(c) from (46)(a) on her own initiative or not, its strength is increased by the fact that (46)(b) is offered as additional evidence for its factuality.

In this case *moreover* is being used to indicate that the utterance it prefaces carries a guarantee of factuality which would not have been carried by the utterance of the preceding sentence alone. The hearer may have recovered the proposition in (49)(c) on her own initiative. What the proposition introduced by *moreover* adds is a licence to assign it a value that would not have been licensed by the utterance of the first sentence. However, it seems that *moreover* may also be used to indicate that the proposition it introduces entitles the hearer to derive a conclusion that she could not have derived at all on the basis of the proposition in the first sentence alone. Consider, for example, the utterance in (50):

(50) Abdul bought a pork chop. Moreover, it was for himself.

The conclusions that the hearer derives from the first proposition will depend on what contextual assumptions she brings to bear. For example, in a context which included (51) the hearer might conclude that Abdul spent a substantial amount of money:

(51) Pork is expensive.

However, the speaker's use of *moreover* indicates that she expects the hearer to process the first proposition of (51) in a context which includes the second proposition. Such a context might be the one in (52):

(52)(a) Muslim dietary law forbids the eating of pork.

(b) Abdul is a Muslim.
(c) Abdul bought the pork for himself.
  (= proposition introduced by *moreover*)

This context allows the hearer to derive the proposition in (52)(d):

(52)(d) Abdul has broken the Muslim dietary law.

The suggestion seems to be that whereas the hearer might have been expected to supply the contextual premises in (52)(a) and (b), she was not expected to supply the premise in (52)(c). However, without this premise the derivation of (52)(d) would have been impossible. In other words, in uttering the second sentence of (50) the speaker has licensed the hearer to derive a conclusion which she assumes would have been otherwise unobtainable.

Consider a further example:

(53) Tom's here. Moreover, he's bought his guitar.

Once again the speaker has used *moreover* to indicate that the proposition it introduces is a premise which is to be combined with the proposition in the first sentence and hence that she is licensing the derivation of a conclusion that would have otherwise been unobtainable. This means that the hearer is expected to perform an inference whose premises include the proposition in the first sentence of (53) and the proposition in the second sentence, together with some other contextual assumptions which can be easily accessed. Now, a hearer could derive a conclusion from the premises in (53) at relatively little cost by accessing a conditional premise of the kind in (54):

(54) If Tom is here and he has brought his guitar, then we can have some music.

In many accounts of inferencing it would be claimed that given a premise of the kind in (54) and the premises in (53), the hearer will derive the conclusion (55) in the following way:

(i) If Tom is here and he has brought his guitar, then we can have some music. (Contextual premise)
(ii) Tom is here. (First proposition of (53))
(iii) Tom has brought his guitar. (Second proposition of (53))

(iv) Tom is here and he has brought his guitar. (*and*-introduction)

---

(55) We can have some music. (*Modus ponendo ponens*)

However, this inference involves the rule of *and*-introduction which according to the arguments outlined in chapter 2, is not part of the deduction system used by hearers in utterance interpretation.

Sperber and Wilson (1986) have shown that, contrary to the views in much of the psychological literature, the rules of *and*-introduction and *or*-introduction are not necessary to account for such examples, since there are psychologically motivated derivations that do not use them. In particular, they point out that any standard logic permits the use of the derived rule in (56):

(56) conjunctive modus ponens
  Input: If (P and Q) then R
   P
  Output: If Q then R

Sperber and Wilson argue that in a relevance-based framework the use of this rule is not just possible, but also highly expected, for it allows inferences to be drawn on the basis of a single conjunct rather than requiring the whole conjunctive antecedent to be supplied. In this way it increases the chance of newly presented information interacting with the hearer's existing representation of the world to enable new conclusions to be drawn.

On the basis of this, I shall assume that the conclusion in (55) will be derived in the following way:

(i) If Tom is here and he has brought his guitar, then we can have some music.
(ii) Tom is here.
(iii) If Tom has brought his guitar, we can have some music. (*Conjunctive modus ponens*)
(iv) Tom has brought his guitar.

---

(55) We can have some music. (*Modus ponendo ponens*)

The main point here, however, is that the proposition introduced by *moreover* is presented as a premise without which the derivation of (55) would not have been possible, or, in other words, that it is the addition of this proposition that entitles the hearer to deduce (55) as a contextual implication.

I have presented (46) and (53) as examples of two different uses of *moreover*. Whereas in (53) *moreover* indicates that the propositions it connects are combined as premises in the same argument, in (46) it indicates that the two propositions are connected by the fact that they are premises for the same conclusion. However, it is clear that there is a common thread running through the accounts of both examples: in both types of case *moreover* indicates that it is the addition of the proposition it introduces that entitles the hearer to process the proposition in the first clause in the way she does. That is, in both cases *moreover* constrains the hearer's choice of context so that the proposition in the first sentence is interpreted as evidence for a specific conclusion.

It will have been recognized that this discussion has been restricted to only one of the expressions of English used to introduce additional evidence. It should be clear that the analyses I have presented for utterances containing *moreover* apply equally to the interpretation of utterances containing *furthermore*. More interestingly, however, all the examples of *moreover* considered here could be replaced by *also*:

(57)(a) Susan has bought a tracksuit. Also she had salad for lunch.
   (b) Tom's here. Also he's brought his guitar.

Also is not, of course, always used in this sentence-initial (and parenthetical) position. However, when it is moved from this position, as in (58) and (59) an extra element may be added to the interpretation process:

(58) Susan bought a chicken and also a chop.
(59) Susan bought a chicken. Ben also bought one.

As we shall see in section 3.5, this element derives from the possibility of *also* interacting with focus.

3.5 Interaction with Focus: 'also'

I concluded section 3.4 by mentioning that although *also* could be used with the equivalent meaning as *moreover*, it has another use, illustrated in (58) and (59) (repeated below), in which an extra element is added to the interpretation process.

(58) Susan bought a chicken and also a chop.
(59) Susan bought a chicken. Ben also bought one.

The difference between these two uses of *also* is reflected in the fact that (60) (b), but not (60) (a) or (c), implies that Ben bought a chicken. (Let the capitalized constituent be the unique focus.)

(60)(a) Susan bought a chicken. Ben bought a CHOP.
   (b) Susan bought a chicken. Ben also bought a CHOP.
        Susan bought a chicken. Moreover/Also, Ben bought a CHOP.

As we shall see, this can be explained by the fact that in contrast with *moreover* and parenthetical/utterance initial *also*, the effect of *also* as it is used in (58) and (59) varies according to which constituent is interpreted as focus. In other words, an account of the role of *also* in these examples must be linked to an account of the way that focal structure affects interpretation.

Before we consider the details of such an account it should be noted that what I have to say about *also* in this use should apply to certain other expressions – notably *too* and *either*. However, my aim here is not so much to give an exhaustive account of these types of expressions as to show how the effect of an inferential constraint on relevance may be amplified through its interaction with focus. This section could, then, be regarded as a suggestion for further research.[8]

It might be thought that in this focal use *also* simply means 'and'. For it would seem that in an utterance such as (58) nothing is implied beyond the assertion that each of the conjuncts is true. On the other hand, if *also* simply indicates that both conjuncts of a conjoined utterance are true, then we ought to be able to insert it in any conjoined utterance without change of acceptability or meaning. The oddity of (61)(a) and (b) suggests that this is not the case:

(61)(a) Ben put his pen to paper and also wrote.
   (b) She dropped the glass and it also broke.

We might explain the oddity of these examples by saying that the effect of *also* is to cancel their temporal and causal connotations.

Similarly, the addition of *also* in (62) (b) seems to cancel the contrastive connotations of (62)(a):[9]

(62)(a) She lives on a farm and he lives in a skyscraper.
   (b) She lives on a farm and he also lives in a skyscraper.

These examples show that *also* makes explicit a relation which cannot be defined in terms of the truth-functional meaning of *and*. As I have said above, we might use the term *addition* to refer to this relation. The problem is that whereas to say that one event took place after another or that one event caused another is clearly to say something other than that both these events took place, it is difficult to see what more is meant by saying that one event took place in addition to another.

The difficulty, then, is that the truth conditions of a conjoined utterance with *also* (for example (58)) are identical to those of a conjoined utterance without *also*. Whatever *also* contributes to the interpretation of these utterances is not truth-conditional, and the relation of addition is not an aspect of their truth-conditional content. This is, of course, consistent with the characterization of *also* as a semantic constraint on relevance.

However, as I have warned, in order to understand the sense in which *also* constrains the relevance of the utterances that contain it, we need to go beyond the roles of such expressions as *after all*, *so*, etc., and consider a different aspect of the way in which the pragmatic interpretation of utterances may be linguistically determined.

A considerable amount of attention has been given in the linguistic and pragmatic literature to the fact that utterances may convey the same information in different ways. For example, while both (63) and (64) entail the propositions in (65), the speaker of (63) will be felt to have taken (65)(b) rather than (65)(a) for granted, while the speaker of (64) will be understood as having taken (65)(a), but not (65)(b) for granted:

(63) It was Susan who bought the chicken.
(64) It was the chicken that Susan bought.
(65)(a) Susan bought something.
   (b) Someone bought the chicken.

This type of phenomenon has been variously described in terms of the distinction between given and new information, topic and comment, theme and rheme, and presupposition and focus. The difficulties associated with these distinctions have been discussed fully by Sperber and Wilson (1986).[10] Here it suffices to say that there are two main problems. First, it is difficult to give adequate criteria for identifying information as, for example, old or as topic. Second, none of the distinctions is accompanied by an adequate account of the role that each type of information plays in utterance interpretation.

Sperber and Wilson analyse the difference between utterances like (63) and (64) in terms of the way they are interpreted as relevant. (For the present purposes it will be sufficient to refer to the version of their account given in Wilson and Sperber, 1979.) Intuitively, whereas in (63) the point of the utterance lies in the identity of the person who bought the chicken, in (64) it lies in the identity of the object Susan bought. Now, it will be recalled that the relevance of a newly presented piece of information depends on the contextual assumptions the hearer supplies as premises for the deduction of its consequences. This means that since each of (63) and (64) expresses exactly the same proposition – (they are true under the same conditions) – the difference in their impact must be due to the fact that this proposition is processed in a different context in each case. The question is, why should this be so?

Wilson and Sperber draw our attention to a particular subset of the entailments of a given proposition, namely, its grammatically specified entailments, or, in other words, the entailments obtained by substituting a logical variable for a syntactic constituent. If we represent these variables by the English proforms *someone*, *something*, *do something*, etc., then we can say that the grammatically specified entailments of (66) include the ones in (67):

(66)   Susan bought a chicken.
(67)(a) Someone bought a chicken.
    (b) Susan bought something.
    (c) Susan did something to a chicken.
    (d) Susan did something.

Wilson and Sperber's first main point is that although the speaker of (66) will have committed herself to the truth of all of the entailments in (67), she will not expect all of them to play the same role in establishing the relevance of the utterance. In their terms, the contextual effects of the utterance will depend on which of these propositions is taken as background. The background does not itself contain the point of the utterance, but rather determines the context in which the relevance of the utterance is established. Thus, for example, to take (67)(a) as background of (66) is to say that the hearer is expected to process the utterance in a context in which it is relevant to know the identity of the person who bought a chicken, while to take (67)(b) as background is to say that the utterance is to be processed in a context in which it is relevant to know what Susan bought. The point of the utterance is the information that has to be added to the background to obtain the proposition as a whole.

The second point made by Wilson and Sperber is that a speaker may use linguistic devices to indicate the pragmatically most important entailments of her utterance. We have already seen in (63) and (64) how clefting serves to highlight a constituent so that it is regarded as containing the point of the utterance. In contrast, a speaker who presents information in an appositive relative clause, as in (68), will indicate that it is not part of the main point of utterance:

(68) Susan, who is having a dinner party, bought a chicken.

However, as they suggest, such devices affect pragmatic interpretation not directly, but through their interaction with stress assignment. It is well known that contrastive stress can affect the pragmatic interpretation of utterances. For example, the heavy stress on *bought* in (69) indicates that the background is the entailment in (67)(c) and hence that the point of the utterance lies in what Susan did with the chicken:

(69) Susan BOUGHT a chicken.

On the other hand, it is equally well known that normal stress is ambivalent in its contribution to utterance interpretation since it does not determine a unique interpretation. Thus, while one can say that the background of an utterance is that entailment obtained by substituting a variable for the constituent stress is used to highlight or focus, a speaker who puts focal stress on *chicken* in (66) may be using it to focus any of the constituents that contain it – that is, the NP *a chicken*, the VP *bought a chicken*, or the S

Susan bought a chicken. Clearly, some account has to be given of how the actual focus is chosen from a range of possible foci. However, the concern of this section is not with stress itself, but with a particular linguistic device which interacts with stress to produce a specific contextual effect.

We have seen that in (69) the contrastive stress on *bought* draws our attention to the fact that the proposition in (67)(c) is being taken for granted and hence that the point of the utterance lies in what Susan did with a chicken. Compare this utterance with the one in (70):

(70) Susan also BOUGHT a chicken.

The speaker of (70) will be understood as having taken for granted not just the proposition in (67)(c), but also the one in (71);

(71) Susan did something else with a chicken.

However, although (71) is clearly assumed by the speaker of (70), it is not a background entailment in the same way that (67)(c) is the background of (69). The hearer is not expected to process (70) in a context in which it is relevant to know what, in addition to buying one, Susan did with a chicken. On the other hand, it is not clear that she is expected to process it simply in a context in which it is relevant to know what Susan did with a chicken on this occasion.

To underline this point further let us compare (72) and (73):

(72) SUSAN bought a chicken.
(73) SUSAN also bought a chicken.

Whereas the speaker of (72) will be felt to have taken just (67)(a) for granted, the speaker of (73) will be understood as having assumed this proposition together with the one in (74):

(74) Someone else bought a chicken.

However, it does not seem we can say that (73) has as its background the conjunction of (67)(a) and (74): the speaker does not think it relevant to know who else bought a chicken and to know who bought one on this occasion. On the other hand, it is clear that the relevance of the utterance does not lie simply in the fact that it was Susan who bought a chicken.

The point is, of course, that no speaker ever produces an utterance like (70) without already having produced – or at least without someone having already produced – an utterance that can be interpreted as providing the value for the variable in (71). That is, (70) is appropriate only in the context of an utterance such as the one in (75):

(75) Susan stole a chicken.

This means that the background of the utterance is the conjunction of (67)(c) and (71), but that the value of the variable in (71) is already in the context. In other words, the hearer is expected to process (70), not in a context in which it is relevant to know what Susan did with a chicken, but rather in one in which it is relevant to know what Susan did with a chicken in addition to whatever she was asserted to have done with a chicken in the previous utterance.

Similarly, (73) is appropriate only in the context of an utterance that supplies the value for the variable in (74) – for example, the one in (76):

(76) Tom bought a chicken.

In this situation the relevance of (73) will be understood to lie in who, in addition to Tom, bought a chicken.

The difference between (70) and (73) is parallel to the difference between (69) and (72): in each case the difference in stress between the two utterances is an indication that they should be interpreted as having a different background, or, in other words, that they are relevant in different contexts. However, whereas (69) and (72) have as their background the grammatically specified entailment obtained by substituting a variable for the focused constituent and are processed in contexts in which it is relevant to know the value of that variable, (70) and (73) are processed in contexts in which it is relevant to know the value of the variable substituted for the focused constituent in addition to the value given to it in the preceding clause.[11]

Why should a speaker indicate that it is relevant to know that one event occurred in addition to another? What, for example, would we gain from the utterance in (77)?

(77) Tom's bought a chicken. Ben has also bought chicken.

This utterance could plausibly be taken to convey the proposition in (78):

(78) We won't be short of chicken tonight.

However, notice that the strength of this conclusion derives from the fact that each of the propositions in (77) provides independent evidence for it. The proposition in (78) may have been derived from the first proposition of (77) alone, but at a strength lower than the strength it receives when given independent confirmation by the presentation of the second proposition. That is, it is relevant to know that chicken was bought by Ben in addition to someone else (Tom) because Ben's purchase provides additional (and hence stronger) confirmation for any conclusion that the hearer might have derived from the fact of Tom's purchase alone. In other words, the function of *also* in this example is the same as that of *moreover*. What the parallelism in focus adds is a more specific indication of the parallelism in the inferential processes involved.

4

Relevance and Coherence: Discourse Connectives

4.1 Coherence in Discourse[1]

Chapter 3 ended with the discussion of an expression whose role as a semantic constraint on relevance is explained in terms of its interaction with such focusing devices as stress. In this chapter I wish to return to the expressions that constrain the interpretation of the utterances that contain them by virtue of the inferential connections they express – *therefore, so, after all, moreover* – and to consider their role as connectives more carefully. In particular, I shall compare the connections they express with the connections recovered from certain utterances with *and*. In this way I hope to be able to characterize the exact sense in which expressions like *after all* and *moreover* may be regarded as discourse connectives.

Much recent work on the interpretation of discourse has adopted the view that the way hearers recover messages from utterances is governed by their assumption that in discourse, contiguous linguistic strings are meant to be interpreted as being connected, or, in other words, that discourse is coherent. These connections are not always made explicit: the hearer is expected to fill them in on the basis of her background or contextual assumptions. Indeed, unless she can recognize that the segments of the discourse cohere in some way, she will not be able to recover any kind of message and the discourse will be ill-formed.

The idea that the elements of a well-formed discourse are bound together by principles of connectivity or textual unity is fundamental to the work of a number of authors – for example, van Dijk (1972), Halliday and Hasan (1976), and Hobbs (1978; 1979).

However, not all these authors agree about the source of the unity. For example, Halliday and Hasan's book is a detailed exploration of the view that a text is created by cohesive relationships within and between sentences – that is, by the use of cohesive devices available in the language. Thus in (1) (a) the 'texture' is created by the use of the pronoun *her* and the ellipse in the second sentence; in (1) (b), apart from the anaphoric relationship between *he* and *his*, there is a cohesive relation expressed by *so*; and in (1) (c) the use of *then* points to a relation of temporal sequence:

(1)(a) My neighbour asked me if I would like to go to her son's school play. I told her I couldn't.
 (b) There was $4 in his wallet. So he hadn't spent all the money.
 (c) I cooked myself an omelette and then spent the evening marking essays.

Halliday and Hasan are careful to point out that a text is a unit of language in use, and, as such, does not consist of sentences. Nevertheless, they claim that the meaning relations within a text are encoded in or realized by sentences: "Cohesion is part of the system of language. The potential for cohesion lies in the systematic resources of reference, ellipsis and so on that are built into the language itself" (1976: 5). However, it is not clear that these meaning relations must be realized explicitly in order for a discourse to have coherence. Both the causal relation expressed in (2)(b) and the temporal relation in (2)(c) could have been conveyed implicitly.[2] Moreover, the relation indicated by a cohesive device is not always a relation between linguistically realized meanings. Recall the situation described in the previous section in which you, on seeing me arrive laden with parcels, produce the utterance in (2):

(2) So you've spent all your money.

It is not clear that a theory of discourse interpretation should distinguish this use of *so* from the one in (1)(b).

Even when two sentences are related by a cohesive tie the hearer has to go beyond his linguistic resources in order to recover an interpretation. For example, Hobbs (1979) points out that in (3) *he* could in principle refer to either John or Bill:

(3) John can open Bill's safe. He knows the combination.

Brown and Yule (1983) suggest that Halliday and Hasan were not attempting to explain how texts are understood, but were instead concerned with the linguistic resources available in English for marking relationships within a text. In other words, they were concerned with cohesion rather than coherence. It is certainly true that a theory of linguistic meaning must take account of those expressions that contribute to the structure and organization of discourse. However, such an account must be grounded in a psychologically adequate theory of the principles by which discourse is organized and understood.

This might suggest that we need to turn to the semantic or conceptual relations that may be realized by cohesive ties, or, in other words, to connectivity of semantic content. Some writers, for example, Hobbs (1978, 1979) and van Dijk (1977), assume that coherence of content can be explicated in terms of coherence relations between propositions. However, Johnson-Laird (1981, 1983) argues that there are two levels of representation for discourse, "a superficial proposition format close to linguistic form, and a mental model that is close to the structure of the events or states of affairs that are described in the discourse" (1983: 377). Coherence relations, he claims, hold between the latter rather than the former. I cannot do justice to Johnson-Laird's arguments for mental models here. However, even without the details of these arguments it seems clear that coherence relations are intended to play the same role in the construction of mental models as the one that, for example, Hobbs attributes to them in the recovery of propositional representations. According to Johnson-Laird, words in a sentence are cues for building a familiar mental model. However, like propositions, mental models are only partially determined by the linguistic properties of utterances. The hearer must use non-linguistic or contextual assumptions in order to construct her model of the state of affairs/event described. The question is, to what extent is the hearer's choice of context, and hence her actual interpretation, determined by her aim of establishing coherence relations?

According to Hobbs, the coherence of a text or discourse is defined in terms of a set of structural binary relations between the segments of a text, which depend on their propositional content. A speaker who wishes her utterance to be understood must ensure that it stands in one of these relations to the preceding text, and that the recognition of the particular relation it bears is essential for its successful comprehension. This approach seems to assume a menu of discourse connections, the speaker's task being to select a connection, and the hearer's task being to identify the speaker's choice. For example, one of the items on Hobbs's menu is the relation of *Elaboration* which subsumes "trivial" moves like pure repetitions, repairs, and tag questions, as well as those cases in which the speaker conveys "the same message from two different perspectives" (1978: 25). It is the recognition of this relation, claims Hobbs, that accounts for the fact that the hearer of (3) above interprets the pronoun *he* as referring to John rather than to Bill.

Now, obviously, discourse is not an arbitrary sequence of utterances. Moreover, hearers are able to identify specific connections between utterances, connections which, as Halliday and Hasan have recognized, may be coded in the language. However, it is clear that a speaker may not use just any coherence relation in order to continue the discourse. Each of the utterances in (4) stands in a coherence relation to the preceding one, and yet the result is nonsense:

(4) John was late. The station clock had struck nine. It was time for Susan to start work. She took the first essay from the pile. It was by Mary Jones. Mary had not been well for weeks. The doctor told her to take a holiday. The problem was that she couldn't afford one. Living in London is now very expensive. All central government subsidies to the Greater London Council have been abolished. Paradoxically, this might be seen to follow from the premises of Libertarian Anarchism. The minor premise might be difficult for the reader to discern. Our theorem proving program does this using a 'crossed-syllogism' technique.

Moreover, as Blass (1985) shows, a text appropriate in one context may be inappropriate in another. The second sentence of (5) can be understood as an Elaboration of the first. While it is appropriate as part of an autobiography, it is inappropriate as part of a *curriculum vitae*:

(5) I was born in Lower Hutt, New Zealand. It used to be a dormitory suburb of Wellington, but is now a busy town with high-rise office blocks.

(Adapted from Blass 1985)

This suggests that a theory of discourse organization cannot consist simply of a taxonomy of coherence relations. It must also include the principles that constrain the speaker's choice of utterance, or, in other words, an account of the appropriateness of utterances in discourse.

Van Dijk (1977) suggests that in order to account for the well-formedness of discourse we need not just an account of the relationships between the sentences of a text, but also an account of the way that each sentence is related to a unifying topic of discourse. According to this view, the problem with a sequence like (4) is that although each sentence is linked to the next by a coherence relation, there is no level of representation (or 'macrostructure') at which the meaning of each sentence defines the meaning of the discourse as a whole.

The notion of topic of discourse (or topic of conversation) is often appealed to, but rarely defined. In his analysis of an example of written text, van Dijk proposes that its topic can be represented as a proposition that is non-trivially and jointly entailed by the ordered sequence of propositions expressed by the sequence of sentences in a text. However, this assumes that the hearer is able to identify the proposition expressed by each sentence in the text. As we have seen, the propositional content of an utterance is only partially determined by its linguistic properties: the actual interpretation recovered by a hearer depends on the non-linguistic or contextual knowledge she brings to bear. Presumably, the hearer's choice of context, and hence her interpretation, is constrained by the requirement that each proposition recovered must be relevant to the topic of the discourse. The problem is that the identification of the discourse topic itself depends on the hearer's ability to recognize the proposition underlying each sentence of the text.

Moreover, as van Dijk himself points out, the context is involved in the recognition of the entailment relations in terms of which the topic of discourse is defined. That is, the topic representation is entailed by the joint set of propositions expressed by the sentences in the text, only given certain items of world knowledge. I mentioned in section 2.4 above that in accounting for such inferences van Dijk appeals to the notion of a frame, that is, a representation of the knowledge people have of stereotypical events and situations. However, as we saw, the notion of a frame itself does not account for the hearer's actual choice of context for the interpretation of an utterance in discourse.

In a coherence-based account of utterance interpretation the role of the context is restricted to establishing coherence relations. However, as Blass (1985) has pointed out, hearers do not always use contextual information in order to maintain coherence relations. She demonstrates this point by appealing to the distinction between the mention and use of language:

(6) A: What did Susan say?
    B: You've dropped your purse.

B's response can be construed either as a report of an assertion made by Susan or as an assertion by B that A has dropped her purse. According to the coherence approach, only the former (coherent) interpretation should be possible. However, it is not difficult to imagine circumstances in which the other non-coherent interpretation would be recovered.

In fact, discourse is full of utterances that do not exhibit coherence relations but are nevertheless perfectly understandable, given the appropriate contextual information. For example, in England, written on a piece of paper attached to an empty milk bottle placed outside someone's front door, (7) will be understood as a request for three pints of milk.

(7) Three bottles today.

In another context, the same piece of paper could convey quite a different message. In other words, the fact that an utterance is neither preceded nor followed by another utterance does not mean that it cannot be understood in isolation from the context. Indeed, as we have seen in (2) above, it is possible that an apparently discourse-initial utterance may be understood only in terms of the specific relationship it bears to information outside the text or discourse. As Blass says, it is not clear why the principles that constrain the selection and use of contextual information in the interpretation of an utterance that is part of a text should be different from the ones that govern its use in the interpretation of an isolated utterance.

Blass's arguments suggest that all discourse, whether it consists of a sequence of utterances or of a single utterance, must be interpreted by the same principles, and that the fact that discourse does not consist of an arbitrary sequence of utterances is a consequence of the fact that speakers aim to conform to them. In the next two sections I shall show how the notion of textual coherence can be derived from the notion of relevance, and hence that it is the relevance-based framework outlined in chapter 2 of this study that provides the most appropriate framework for the explanation of cohesive ties in discourse.

4.2 Coherence and Content: The Interpretation of Conjoined Utterances

Coherence is defined as a relationship between linguistic units – that is, utterances or the segments of a text. By contrast, relevance is defined in terms of a relationship between propositions. As we have seen, a proposition may be relevant whether or not it has been deliberately communicated. It does not matter whether you tell me that the milk is boiling over or whether I discover the fact for myself. Either way the information is relevant to me if there is a small and immediately accessible context in which it has contextual effects. This is not to say that we cannot talk of the relevance of an utterance. But this is a derivative notion: an utterance is relevant only in the sense that it conveys relevant information.

Turning to the other side of the relationship, the context used in establishing the relevance of a proposition is not, as in the coherence-based accounts, simply characterized as the co-text of discourse, but as a set of assumptions stored in memory. Again, this is not to say that an earlier utterance or text segment cannot make assumptions for the interpretation of an utterance available. Indeed, as we shall see in this section and in section 4.3, this is what characterizes a coherent text. However, contextual assumptions may also be derived from a non-communicative event – that is, from observation of the environment.

It will be recalled that the Principle of Relevance entitles the hearer to interpret every utterance in the smallest and most immediately accessible context to yield an adequate range of contextual effects. In general, this will mean that an utterance will be interpreted in the context made available by the most recently processed proposition, which in connected discourse will be the one expressed by the previous utterance or text segment. In other words, in the relevance-based framework of the present study the appropriateness of an utterance in discourse depends on the possibility of establishing a connection between it and the preceding utterance only in the sense that the interpretation of the latter yields assumptions that are used in the interpretation of the former.

Now, we have seen in chapter 1 of this study that contextual assumptions are required not only for establishing the implicit (non-truth-conditional) import of an utterance – for instance, its contextual implications – but also for establishing its propositional (truth-conditional) content. This would seem to suggest that on the relevance-based approach we can distinguish two kinds of coherence in discourse: (a) the coherence that arises when information made available by the interpretation of one segment of discourse is used in establishing the propositional content of the next; and (b) the coherence that arises when the information made available by the interpretation of one discourse segment is used in establishing the contextual effects of the next. One of my aims in this chapter is to present a set of facts whose explanation hinges on the distinction between these two types of coherence. First, however, let us consider some examples of the first type.

Consider how a hearer would interpret the pronoun *it* in each of the following:

(8)   A: Have you heard Periah's recording of the Moonlight Sonata?
      B: Yes, it made me realize that I'd never be able to perform it.

(Adapted from Maclaran 1982)

(9)   I put the butterfly wing on the table. It broke.

(10)   I put the heavy book on the table. It broke.
(Both adapted from Boden 1977: 174)

I have chosen these examples because in each case there is no linguistic rule whose application would enable the hearer to recover the correct interpretation. This is only recovered on the basis of contextual (that is, non-linguistic) information made available by the interpretation of the first segment in the sequence in accordance with the Principle of Relevance. Thus, for example, in the sequence in (8) A's utterance makes available two possible referents for each of the occurrences of *it* in B's utterance: the recording and the sonata. The hearer's task is to decide which referent must be assigned to each occurrence of the pronoun. Clearly, the only interpretation to yield any contextual effects is the one in which the first instance is construed as the recording and the second as the sonata.

The problem in (9) and (10) should be apparent from the contrasting interpretations. In each case the most relevant interpretation of the second segment involves the establishment of a causal connection between the event it describes and the one described in the first. However, whereas the first segment of (9) gives the hearer access to information (about the fragility of butterfly wings) which yields an interpretation in which the butterfly wing was caused to break, the first segment of (10) gives him access to information (about the weight of the book) which yields the interpretation in which the table was caused to break.

The suggestion of causal sequence in these last two examples brings me to the interpretation of conjoined utterances, which, as is well known, often have causal connotations. A number of writers, following Grice, have argued that the causal connotations of conjoined utterances such as (11) cannot be due to the meaning of *and*, since the same connotations can be recovered from the corresponding non-co-ordinated, or as I shall call it, *full-stop* utterance – in this case the utterance in (12):

(11)   The road was icy and she slipped.
(12)   The road was icy. She slipped.

The conclusion drawn from such examples is that the causal connotations of both conjoined and full-stop utterances are due to general pragmatic principles and hence must be analysed as conversational implicatures.

There are two important assumptions underlying this argument. First, it is assumed that anything that is pragmatically determined is a conversational implicature – or, in other words, that pragmatic principles do not play a role in the recovery of what is said. Second, it is assumed that pragmatic principles apply to full-stop utterances in the same way that they apply to conjoined utterances.

We have already seen that the first of these assumptions cannot be maintained. Pragmatic principles must play a role in disambiguation, reference assignment, the resolution of vagueness, and the recovery of ellipsed or unexpressed material. In this section we shall consider how the idea that there are pragmatically determined aspects of propositional content applies to the interpretation of conjoined utterances. In section 4.3 I shall turn to the second assumption and show that although it is true that the suggestions of temporal and causal sequence conveyed by conjoined utterances may also be conveyed by full-stop utterances, there are suggestions conveyed by the latter that may not be conveyed by the former.

As I have said, the analysis of the temporal and causal connotations of conjoined utterances as implicatures has the advantage of allowing a unitary and truth-functional analysis of the meaning of *and*. Thus, for example, we do not need to postulate an extra non-truth-functional 'and then' sense for *and* in order to account for the suggestion conveyed by (13) that he jumped after he ran over to the cliff:

(13)   He ran over to the cliff and jumped.

It is an implicature due to the assumption that the Maxim of Manner has been observed and the speaker is presenting the events in the order in which they occurred. A similar point applies to the earlier example in (11), although in this case the implicature would follow from the assumption that the speaker was being relevant.

However, as Cohen (1971) has shown, this analysis is inconsistent with the fact that both temporal and causal suggestions can fall under the scope of logical operators. Thus, for example, the fact that neither of the utterances in (14) and (15) is redundant or semantically anomalous suggests that the causal and temporal suggestions conveyed by their embedded clauses must be treated as contributing to the truth conditions of the utterance as a whole:

(14) If the old king has died of a heart attack and a republic was declared, then Sam will be happy, but if a republic was declared and the king died of a heart attack then Sam will be unhappy. (Adapted from Cohen 1971)
(15) It's always the same at parties: either you get drunk and no-one will talk to you or no-one will talk to you and you get drunk. (From Carston 1985)

Cohen takes such examples to be evidence against the implicature account in favour of the 'semantic ambiguity' account in which *and* means 'and then' and 'and as a result' in addition to its truth-functional sense. However, the fact that these suggestions can be cancelled without contradiction has led Carston (1984) to offer an alternative account in which they are analysed as pragmatically determined elements of propositional content. It will be recalled that Wilson and Sperber (1981) showed that the propositional content of an utterance may be under-determined by its linguistic content not only in the sense that contextual information is required for the assignment of reference and for disambiguation, but also in the sense that the meanings of the words uttered may determine a proposition too under-specified to be taken as the one the speaker could have intended. In chapter 1 this point was illustrated by the example repeated here as (16) where the hearer's search for relevance leads her to recover the much more completely specified proposition in (17):

(16) It will take us some time to get there.
(17) It will take us longer to get there than you think.

In applying this idea to the analysis of the temporal connotations of conjoined utterances Carston makes the quite standard assumption that an utterance describing an event is interpreted as expressing a proposition which contains a value for a time index determined on the basis of the context. Her point is that, given her background beliefs and the Principle of Relevance, the hearer can go beyond the linguistic meaning of an utterance like (13) and recover values for the time index in each conjunct so that if the value of the index in the first conjunct is t, then the value for the index in the second conjunct is $t+n$. Thus the proposition recovered from (13) may be represented as in (18):

(18) He ran over to the cliff at t and he jumped at $t+n$

This account seems to echo a claim made by Fodor and Fodor (1980) that if someone does something, then there is a time, place, and manner in which he does it. This is not meant to apply at the level of grammatical representation: It does not mean, for example, that the grammatical representation for (13) must include an empty PP slot. Rather it applies at the level of propositional representation (or in the Language of Thought). But while it is true that a hearer may go beyond the linguistic content of an utterance and supply information of this sort, it is not true that she will do this in every case. It all depends on whether it is worth her while – that is, on whether the information is optimally relevant. Fodor and Fodor make their claim specifically about drinking and eating. In fact, the main point of their paper was to provide a semantic account of the interpretation of utterances containing verbs that can appear with or without an overt direct object. In this account there is a meaning postulate associated with the predicate DRINK which licenses the hearer to infer from a proposition of the form in (19)(a) a proposition of the form in (19)(b):

(19)(a) x DRINK
  (b) $\exists y(x$ DRINK $y)$

However, once again the inference made is constrained by the Principle of Relevance. Wilson and Sperber (1979) have already shown that the Principle of Relevance may entitle the hearer to derive a much more completely specified proposition than the one he would recover on the basis of Fodor and Fodor's meaning postulates. For example, the suggestion in (20) is not that there was something that the king drank, but that the king drank the wine:

(20) The king picked up the wine and drank.

That is, the hearer's search for relevance will lead her to recover the proposition represented in (21):

(21) [The king]$_i$ picked up [the wine]$_j$ at t and he$_i$ drank it$_j$ at $t+n$.

More generally, the optimally relevant interpretation of a conjoined utterance may go beyond its linguistic content so that its second conjunct includes information determined by the interpretation of the first. This approach allows us to account for a wide range of suggestions, including the suggestion in (13) that he jumped off the cliff.[3] However, perhaps most important from the point of view of the present section is that it allows us to account for the interpretation of the causal connotations of utterances like (11). The fact that an event occurred does not entail that it had a cause. Nevertheless, the optimally relevant interpretation of a conjoined utterance may be one whose second conjunct contains a causal predicate (an AS A RESULT OF predicate) whose argument is determined by the interpretation of the first conjunct. Thus the hearer of (11) will interpret it as expressing the proposition in (22):

(22) [The road was icy]$_i$ and as a result of that$_i$ she slipped.

According to this account, the causal and temporal connotations of conjoined utterances are examples of the connections that characterize any coherent discourse. That is, they arise from the way that information made available by the interpretation of one discourse segment is used in establishing the propositional content of the next. It is not surprising, then, that these suggestions can be conveyed either by conjoined utterances or by full-stop utterances, as, for example, in (12). However, it should not be concluded from this that conjoined utterances and full-stop utterances are processed for relevance in the same way. For there are connections that can be conveyed by full-stop utterances that cannot be conveyed by the corresponding conjoined utterance. Consider, for example, the sequence in (23):

(23) She slipped. The road was icy.

This example is adapted from one noted by H. Clark (cited by Gazdar 1979: 44), who took it to be a counter-example to Grice's Maxim of Manner since the normal temporal and causal connotations cannot be recovered. What this example suggests, of course, is that the fact of there being ice on the road is an explanation for her having slipped, a suggestion which, as we saw in chapter 3, may be made explicit by the use of the expression *you see*:

(24) She slipped. You see, the road was icy.

As Gazdar points out, this suggestion cannot be conveyed by a conjoined utterance: (25) conveys nothing beyond the truth of each of its conjuncts:

(25) She slipped and the road was icy.

This would seem to suggest that whereas the Maxim of Manner (and in particular the sub-maxim 'Be orderly') always applies to conjoined utterances, it does not always apply to full-stop utterances.

At this point an advocate of the ambiguity or semantic analysis of conjoined utterances might say that the discrepancy between (11) and (25) is due to the fact that the meaning of *and* is such that it does not allow the hearer to interpret its arguments as effect and cause, but only as cause and effect. That is, whereas *and* means either 'and then' or 'and as a result' or '&' (i.e. truth-functional *and*), fullstop does not mean anything, and the hearer is free to interpret the propositions presented either as cause and effect or as effect and cause, his choice being governed by pragmatic principles.

In fact, I am going to accept the view that *and* is not equivalent to fullstop. However, I do not wish to suggest that it has 'as a result' as one of its meanings. Indeed, as we shall see, the discrepancy between (11) and (25) can be explained without attributing to *and* any meaning beyond its standard truth-functional one. As we shall see, the key to this explanation lies in the way these utterances are processed for relevance, and in particular, to the distinction between the two types of coherence drawn at the beginning of this section.

4.3 Coherence and Relevance: Inferential Connections

According to the discussion so far, both of the following utterances are interpreted as suggesting a causal connection between the icy state of the road and the fact that she slipped:

(26) The road was icy and she slipped. (=11)
(27) She slipped. The road was icy. (=25)

The problem is that whereas the suggestion recovered from (26) can be conveyed either by a conjoined utterance or by the corresponding fullstop utterance, the one recovered from (27) can be conveyed only by a fullstop utterance. Intuitively, it seems that this discrepancy must be due to the fact that whereas in (26) the suggestion arises in the course of a narrative, in (27) it is part of an explanation. In other words, the conjuncts of a conjoined utterance, in contrast to the segments of a fullstop utterance cannot be related as the elements in an explanation. But why should this be so?

In section 4.2 it was argued that the suggestion of causal sequence conveyed by a conjoined utterance is a pragmatically determined aspect of propositional content. That is, it is an example of the way in which hearers enrich the propositional content of utterances in accordance with their aim of maximizing relevance. In contrast, the suggestion conveyed by (27) is an assumption which the hearer is expected to supply in order to establish the second proposition as an explanation for the event described by the first. That is, it is a premise which licenses the inference from the proposition that the road was icy to the proposition that she slipped.

However, the fact that the connection in (27) is an inferential connection is not in itself an explanation for the oddity of the corresponding conjoined utterance. For as I mentioned in chapter 3, inferential connections can be conveyed by conjoined utterances, whether explicitly, as in (28), or implicitly, as in (29):

(28) Conjoined utterances convey suggestions of temporal sequence and so *and* is not truth-functional.
(29) If conjoined utterances convey suggestions of temporal sequence and *and* is not truth-functional, then you will have to revise your theory.

The inferential connections that may be conveyed by conjoined utterances also include the one expressed by *moreover* and *furthermore*:

(30) Susan voted for the strike and, furthermore, she's a member of the Socialist Workers Party.

The problem is that they do not include the connection expressed by *you see* or, indeed, the one expressed by *after all*. Thus the utterance in (31) is unacceptable and in (32) it is impossible to interpret the second conjunct as evidence for the first:

(31) Jane can add up the bill and after all, she's a mathematician.
(32) Jane can add up the bill and she's a mathematician.

As we have seen, the Principle of Relevance provides the hearer with a guarantee that the speaker has aimed to produce an utterance that yields adequate contextual effects at a minimum cost in processing. That is, given the Principle of Relevance, the hearer is entitled to expect that any effort expended in processing an utterance is offset by some contextual effect. This means that a hearer who is presented with a conjoined utterance cannot be expected to undertake the processing entailed by the use of *and* unless the conjoined proposition that is expressed has relevance over and above the relevance of each conjunct taken individually. What otherwise would be the point of producing the conjoined utterance in the first place? This is not to say that each conjunct may not have its own individual relevance. The point is simply that the hearer of a conjoined utterance receives no guarantee that each of the conjuncts is relevant. She can only assume that it is the conjoined proposition that is consistent with the Principle of Relevance.[4]

In some cases the relevance of the conjoined proposition may simply lie in the fact that it is a list. Consider, for example, (33) and (34):

(33) Wellington is in the North Island and Christchurch is in the South Island.
(34) I wrote some letters and painted the ceiling.

One of the reasons for producing a list rather than a sequence of isolated propositions is to provide a single answer to a single (implicit or explicit) question – for example, 'Where are the chief towns in New Zealand?' or 'What did you do in the weekend?' – so that the relevance of the utterance hinges on the fact that each conjunct is interpreted against the same set of contextual assumptions. Notice here that there is a sense in which the conjuncts of (29) could be regarded as items on a list. For the use of *furthermore* indicates that the two propositions are items on a list of premises which taken together provide more evidence for a given conclusion than each proposition taken individually.

Returning to the examples in (33) and (34), it will be recognized that (34) may not necessarily be interpreted simply as a list. It may be taken to convey a suggestion of temporal sequence, in which case the hearer will treat the first conjunct as contributing towards, and thus modifying, the context for the interpretation of the second. As we have seen, the hearer's decision to interpret a conjoined utterance in this way is governed by her aim of maximizing relevance. If the linguistic properties of the utterance (together with the ascription of reference) do not determine a sufficiently relevant proposition, then the hearer may go beyond the linguistic meaning to recover a far more completely specified proposition. The point here is that the hearer's aim, when she is presented with a conjoined utterance such as (34) is to recover a maximally relevant conjoined proposition – one that has relevance over and above that of its individual conjuncts.

It seems that the search for relevance may lead the hearer of a conjoined utterance to enrich its content so that it includes an inferential connection of the kind expressed by *so*. For in certain cases this connection may fall under the scope of logical operators. Recall, for example, the conditional in (29):

(29) If conjoined utterances convey suggestions of temporal sequence and (so) *and* is not truth functional, then you will have to revise your theory.

If the two conjuncts of the antecedent are both true, but it is not the case that the second follows from the first, then even if it is true that the addressee has to revise her theory, the conditional will be false. This is not to say that *so* is itself ambiguous between the non-truth-conditional sense described in chapter 3 and a further truth-conditional sense. The use of *so*, as always, instructs the hearer to establish an inferential connection. The fact that this connection is interpreted as part of the propositional content of an utterance like (29) is due to the same factor that leads any hearer to enrich the content of a conjoined utterance – the assumption that it expresses a conjoined proposition which is consistent with the Principle of Relevance.

The picture of discourse that emerges from the relevance-based framework adopted in this book is one in which the interpretation of an utterance (that is, its propositional content and its contextual effects) contributes towards the context for interpreting subsequent utterances. That is, as discourse proceeds, the hearer is provided with a gradually changing background against which new information is processed. As we have seen interpreting an utterance involves more than identifying the proposition it expresses. It also involves working out the consequences of adding it to the hearer's existing assumptions, or, in other words, working out its relevance. In this framework, then, the context can be viewed from either of two perspectives. On the one hand, it may be regarded as the set of assumptions used in establishing the relevance of a new item of information, while on the other, it may be seen as the set of assumptions that is modified or affected by the presentation of a new item of information. A new item of information may affect a context by virtue of adding to it. However, it may also have a contextual effect by virtue of providing evidence for an existing assumption or alternatively against an existing assumption. This means that in a coherent discourse two utterances may be connected either in virtue of the fact that the interpretation of the first may include propositions used in establishing the relevance of the second, or in virtue of the fact that a proposition conveyed by one is affected by the interpretation of the other. In either case we might say that the relevance of one is somehow *dependent* on the interpretation of the other.

It will be recalled that in Sperber and Wilson's (1986) framework the processes involved in working out the relevance of a newly presented proposition are crucially inferential. Given the role of inference in establishing the contextual effects of a proposition, it should not be surprising that expressions that instruct the hearer to establish an inferential connection between two segments of discourse may be used to indicate how the proposition they introduce is to be interpreted as relevant. That is, it should not be surprising that expressions like *so, moreover, you see*, and *after all* can be used to express relationships of dependent relevance.

This, of course, was the role of these expressions discussed in chapter 3. However, my concern there was to show not only that the role of these expressions as semantic constraints on relevance followed from the role of inference in pragmatic interpretation, but also that the existence of these constraints can be explained in terms of the speaker's goal of optimizing relevance in accordance with the Principle of Relevance, or, in other words, of ensuring correct context selection at minimal processing cost. Indeed, given Sperber and Wilson's framework, it is difficult to see why a speaker would direct the hearer to a specific interpretation for a proposition unless she was aiming to produce an utterance consistent with the Principle of Relevance. This means that if an expression has been used to constrain the relevance of the proposition it introduces, then that proposition must be consistent with the Principle of Relevance. If, as I have argued, the conjuncts of the conjoined proposition expressed by a conjoined utterance cannot be consistent with the Principle of Relevance individually, then the use of *so* and *moreover* in (27), (28), and (29) above cannot be analysed in terms of dependent relevance. That is, they cannot be analysed as imposing constraints on the propositions they introduce, but must rather contribute to the interpretation of the conjoined proposition as a whole.

Notice that this means that the second proposition of (28) and (29) cannot be relevant as a specification of the relevance of the first proposition. For then the two propositions would have to be consistent with the Principle of Relevance individually. By the same token, it follows that the connection expressed by *you see* could never be conveyed in a conjoined utterance. For according to the analysis in chapter 3, the proposition introduced by *you see* must be relevant as an explanation. That is, it is relevant as an answer raised by the presentation of the first proposition. And, of course, questions and answers are by their very nature planned as separate utterances, each one satisfying the Principle of Relevance individually. The same point applies to the connection expressed by *after all*. The need for a justification must have already been created – for example, by a previous utterance. But to say that the relevance of a proposition depends on the presentation of another is to say that each is consistent with the Principle of Relevance individually. As we have seen, although the two conjuncts of a conjoined utterance may have their own individual relevance, it is only the conjoined proposition whose relevance is guaranteed under the Principle of Relevance.

In these last two sections I have distinguished between two kinds of coherence. On the one hand, there is the coherence that arises when the interpretation of one segment of discourse is used in establishing the content of the next. On the other, there is the coherence that I have analysed as dependent relevance. Clearly, there can be connectivity of content within utterances as well as between utterances. In particular, there can be connectivity of content within conjoined utterances. However, as I have attempted to show, to say that two segments of discourse are connected in the sense that the relevance of one is dependent on the other is to say that each is consistent with the Principle of Relevance individually. Accordingly, we might expect to find relations of dependent relevance holding between segments of discourse that express different propositional attitudes and between segments produced by different speakers. On the other hand, for the reasons just discussed, we do not expect such relations to hold between the conjuncts of a conjoined utterance.

As readers will be aware, both types of coherence may be made explicit by the use of certain lexical items. For example, the connectivity of content that gives rise to temporal connotations of conjoined utterances may be made explicit by the use of expressions like *then*. The fact that such an expression contributes to the coherence of discourse might seem to suggest that it is as much a *discourse connective* as the expressions discussed in chapter 3. On the other hand, to describe these expressions as discourse connectives would be to obscure not only the distinction between the two different types of coherence, but also the distinction that gave rise to this book. Since, as we have seen, temporal and causal connotations are part of the propositional content over which pragmatic computations are defined, expressions like *then* and *as a result* must be part of logical form. That is, they must be part of the linguistic representation that is developed into a propositional representation on the basis of the context and the Principle of Relevance. In contrast, the connection expressed by, for example, *after all*, is not part of a propositional representation over which pragmatic computations are defined, but arises out of the way that one proposition is interpreted as relevant with respect to another. That is, *after all* is not part of a linguistic representation which is developed into a proposition, but imposes a constraint on the pragmatic computations a proposition may enter into. Accordingly, I would like to suggest that if the term *discourse connective* is to have any theoretical significance at all, it should be reserved for the description of those expressions used to indicate how the relevance of one discourse segment is dependent on another.

4.4 *But*: Denial and Conjunction

In the final two sections of this study I discuss the implications of the framework I have been developing for what is perhaps the most notorious example of a word whose meaning cannot be defined in truth-conditional terms. It is generally assumed that *but* has part of its meaning in common with *and*, so that an utterance like (35) is true if and only if both conjuncts are true:

(35) Tom has come but he has brought his dog.

However, it is also recognized that utterances with *but* have contrastive connotations often lacking in utterances with *and*. Compare, for example, (35) and (36):

(36) Tom has arrived and he has brought his dog.

This has been taken to suggest that *but* means 'and + something else.' However, attempts to distinguish *but* from *and* by writing a semantics for the 'something else' have generally met with serious difficulties. In the first place, many writers have found it necessary to distinguish between two uses of *but*: the so-called 'denial of expectation' use illustrated in (37) and the so-called 'contrast' use illustrated in (38):

(37) John is a Republican but he's honest.
(38) Susan is tall but Mary is short.

R. Lakoff (1971) presented this distinction as a distinction between two meanings of *but*, a proposal found unsatisfactory by, for example, Kempson (1975) and Dascal and Katriel (1977). Although it is nowadays accepted that *but* is not semantically ambiguous, little progress has been made in formulating a description of its meaning that unites all of its uses.

A further difficulty arises from the need to make reference to the context in accounting for the suggestion that *but* conveys. In R. Lakoff's account the context only plays a role in the interpretation of denial of expectation *but*. Hence her term *semantic contrast*. However, as we shall see, it is not legitimate to distinguish between two *but*s on these grounds. One might conclude from this – as, indeed, R. Lakoff (1971) and G. Lakoff (1970, 1971) have done – that a distinction between semantics and pragmatics cannot be maintained, at least as a distinction between linguistic meaning and contextually determined meaning. In this section I shall take the fact that the meaning of *but* interacts with the context not as evidence for the conflation of linguistic meaning and pragmatically determined meaning, but rather as evidence that the pragmatic interpretation of utterances may be constrained by linguistic means. As I have shown in chapter 3, the existence of linguistically specified structures which constrain the contexts in which utterances containing them can occur can only be explained given a coherent and psychologically adequate account of the role of the context in interpretation. As Sperber and Wilson (1986) have shown, such an account is possible, only given a principled distinction between linguistic knowledge and non-linguistic (or contextual) knowledge.

What I am going to argue, then, is that the meaning of *but* must be analysed not in terms of its contribution to the truth-conditional or propositional content of the utterances that contain it, but as a purely non-truth-conditional constraint on relevance (in the sense defined in chapter 3). This analysis is in direct conflict with the traditional view that *but* has 'and' as part of its meaning, a view which I shall show does not take account of either the pragmatic interpretation of conjoined utterances or the meaning of *but*.

I say 'the meaning of *but*'. This is perhaps misleading in that I cannot promise a precise description of the core common to all uses of *but*. However, I do hope to show that given a proper appreciation of the notions of denial and contrast, it is possible to see that the only sense in which *but* indicates contrast is one that involves denial, and that the difference between the two uses lies in the role that the first proposition of a pair connected by *but* plays in establishing that the second is a denial. I shall begin, then, with denial.

According to the pragmatic theory outlined in chapter 2, a hearer is entitled to approach the interpretation of every utterance on the assumption that it will result in some contextual effect, some improvement to her overall representation of the world. As we have seen, this does not mean necessarily that speakers simply aim to give hearers more information about the world. The effect of an utterance may be to provide better evidence for assumptions the hearer already holds. Indeed, a hearer's representation of the world may be said to have been improved by the elimination of an assumption. In chapter 3 we considered expressions whose meanings interacted with inference in its role as a means of assessing the extent to which a new item of information provides evidence for an existing assumption. The basic idea there was that assumptions about the world come with varying degrees of strength, and that logical computations assign strength to conclusions on the basis of the strength of the premises from which they are derived. In this framework a proposition whose presentation enables a hearer to derive an assumption which she has already represented may be relevant in virtue of strengthening the hearer's conviction that it is true: having two independent pieces of evidence for an assumption will lead a hearer to assign it a degree of strength which is greater than she would have done on the basis of each piece of evidence individually.

In this section we shall be concerned with the role played by inference in establishing that a new item of information is relevant by virtue of the fact that it leads the hearer to abandon an existing assumption. Let us recall the situation described in chapter 2 in which I have some reason to believe that you speak Russian – perhaps I saw you once carrying some books with Russian titles from the library. However, during a discussion at a party I hear you produce the utterance in (39):

(39) I wish I could speak Russian.

This utterance conveys a proposition which contradicts my original assumption. The fact that I cannot hold both assumptions means that I must abandon one of them. As we saw, in the situation described, it is clear which of the two assumptions I am likely to retain. The fact that you produced the utterance in (39) provides me with stronger evidence for the proposition it conveys than I have for my original assumption. Accordingly, I shall abandon the latter in favour of the former. In other words, when it is possible to compare the relative strength of two contradictory assumptions, it is possible to resolve the contradiction by abandoning the one for which there is less support.

Now, obviously, one would not want to describe your utterance as a denial. It is not clear precisely what contextual effects you thought you would achieve. It is quite possible that you have no grounds for thinking that your utterance was relevant by virtue of any one specific contextual effect. Nevertheless it is unlikely that the denial of my assumption was amongst the range of implicated contextual effects that you might have expected to achieve. This does not detract from the effect that it did in fact have for me. The point is that there was no reason for you to think that this was the optimally relevant interpretation, or, in other words, that this would be the way in which your utterance achieved optimal relevance.

The suggestion, then, is that we reserve the term 'denial' for those utterances in which it is assumed that the speaker has grounds for thinking that the optimally relevant interpretation yields a proposition inconsistent with an assumption held by the hearer. Notice that an utterance may be a denial either in virtue of its propositional (explicit) content or in virtue of its implicated (or implicit) content or in virtue of its implicated (or implicit) content. Let us call B's response to A in (40) a direct denial and C's response an indirect denial:

(40) A: Ben isn't at work today.
      B: Yes, he is.
      C: I just saw him in his office.

Neither B nor C need give any linguistic indication as to the way in which she expects her utterance to be interpreted: given that she has good grounds for thinking that the hearer has immediate access to the proposition expressed by A's utterance, she has good grounds for thinking this is the most immediately accessible interpretation. Still, it will be recognized that even in this type of situation a speaker (particularly a speaker of an indirect denial) may preface her utterance with *but* (although, interestingly, not with any other so-called contrastive particles like *however* and *nevertheless*).

This is not, of course, the kind of case that has most interested those working on the semantics of *but*. The denial typically associated with so-called 'denial of expectation' *but* is a denial – either direct, as in (37), or indirect, as in (41) – of a proposition which, although not part of the propositional content of the sentence just uttered, is understood as being part of its interpretation.

(41) [A and B are discussing the economic situation and decide that they should consult a specialist in economics]
A: John is an economist.
B: He is not an economist but he is a businessman.

Example (37) may be recognized as that of G. Lakoff (1971); (41) is taken from Dascal and Katriel (1977), who use it to show that Lakoff's account of denial of expectation *but* should be extended to cover those cases in which the proposition introduced by *but* implies a proposition inconsistent with a proposition understood to have been conveyed in preceding clause. In each case the hearer is expected to be able to supply the appropriate contextual assumptions in order to establish the inconsistency. Thus in (37) the hearer is expected to combine the proposition in the first clause with the contextual assumption in (42)(a) in order to derive the proposition in (42)(b), which is then explicitly denied by the *but*-clause.

(42)(a) All Republicans are dishonest.
   (b) John is dishonest.

The reasoning in (41) is more complicated. The hearer is expected to derive (43)(b) from the first clause on the basis of the contextual premise in (43)(a). (43)(b) is not inconsistent with the proposition expressed by the *but*-clause, but with the proposition in (44)(b) which the hearer is expected to have derived on the basis of the contextual assumption in (44)(a):

(43)(a) If John isn't an economist, then we shouldn't seek his opinion.
   (b) We shouldn't seek John's opinion.
(44)(a) If John is a businessman, then we should seek his opinion.
   (b) We should seek John's opinion.

It is a relatively straightforward matter to accommodate this use of *but* in the framework I have developed for other semantic constraints on relevance: in (37) and (41) *but* constrains the interpretation of the proposition it introduces so that its relevance must be understood to lie in its effect on the interpretation of the proposition in the preceding clause. More specifically, the hearer is instructed to process the proposition *but* introduces in a context in which she can derive a proposition logically inconsistent with one assumed to have been derived from the proposition expressed by the utterance of the first clause. Notice that a speaker may use *but* to indicate that the proposition it introduces is relevant by virtue of being inconsistent with a proposition understood to have been conveyed by an utterance made by another speaker. That is, there is no reason why in (41) the *but* clause may not have been uttered by another speaker, as in (45):

(45) B: John is not an economist.
      C: But he is a businessman.

There is no temptation here, I believe, to say that *but* has 'and' as part of its meaning. B's utterance and C's response are connected in some sense, but not in the sense of being constituents of a conjoined proposition. However, this connection is exactly the same as the connection between the two components of B's utterance in (41). If the two propositions in (45) are not connected as conjuncts of a conjoined proposition, then why should they be connected in this way in (41)?

In section 4.3 I suggested that a speaker aiming at optimal relevance could not expect the hearer to undertake the processing entailed by her use of *and* unless she had grounds for thinking that the conjoined proposition had relevance over and above the relevance of its conjuncts taken individually. That is, the speaker of a conjoined utterance gives a guarantee that it is the conjoined proposition it expresses that is consistent with the Principle of Relevance. In contrast, according to the analysis just given, a speaker uses *but* in order to constrain the relevance of the proposition it introduces, or, in other words, to indicate how that proposition satisfies the Principle of Relevance. As we have seen, the description of that constraint makes reference to the proposition expressed in the preceding clause. But the point was that the connection was one between the pragmatic interpretation of one proposition and the pragmatic interpretation of another, or, in other words, between two propositions, each of which is consistent with the Principle of Relevance individually.

Hearers do not always have to be instructed how to process a proposition for relevance – particularly when the required contextual assumptions are made accessible through the interpretation of the immediately preceding discourse. Recall, for instance, the dialogue in (40). However, in the case of (37), (41), and (45) the connection between the two propositions has to be made explicit by the use of *but*. Compare, for example, (37) with (46):

(46) John is a Republican. He is honest.

Here there are all sorts of less costly ways in which the hearer can establish the relevance of the second proposition in a context made accessible by the first. It may be relevant as evidence for the truth of the first proposition, or, alternatively, as an explanation for its truth. This suggests that if it hadn't been for the use of *but* in (37) the hearer might never have accessed the assumption in (42)(a) and derived the conclusion in (42)(b). In other words, in indicating how the proposition it introduces is relevant, the speaker's use of *but* also indicates how she expects the first proposition might have been interpreted.

4.5 *But*: Contrast and Conjunction

The observation made at the end of the previous section seems to provide us with a basis for distinguishing between two *but*s. For it appears that the suggestion conveyed by the so-called contrast *but* can be conveyed implicitly. Thus for example, it could be claimed that (47) conveys implicitly what (38) conveys explicitly:

(47) Susan is tall. Mary is short.

Perhaps more significantly still, it appears that, unlike the suggestion conveyed by the use of denial *but*, that one conveyed by contrast *but* can be conveyed implicitly in a conjoined utterance. Compare (48) with (38) and (49) with (37):

(48) Susan is tall and Mary is short.
(49) John is a Republican and he is honest.[5]

In this section I hope to show that while (47) and (48) may indeed be interpreted as conveying a suggestion of contrast, they are not always interpreted in the same way as the corresponding utterances with *but*.

It might be thought that in these examples the contrast is evident from the semantic properties of the words used: *tall* and *short* are the opposite extremes of a continuous scale. That is, they are gradable antonyms. However, not all examples of contrast involve antonymy. In (50) the predicates merely represent different values on a continuous scale:

(50)   Susan is tall. Anne is of average height.

And in some cases, for example in (51), the predicates contrast simply in virtue of representing properties understood as being part of a system of mutual incompatibles:

(51)   The onions are fried. The cabbage is steamed.

Indeed, in many cases there does not seem to be any semantic incompatibility at all. It is possible for someone to own a Porsche and a Mini, and liking skiing does not rule out playing chess. Nevertheless (52) and (53) may be understood to convey a contrast.

(52)   Mary likes skiing. Anne plays chess.
(53)   His father owns a Mini. Mine has a Porsche.

It may be recalled that it was cases such as these that led R. Lakoff to stretch the notion of antonymy so that, for example, we could say that *skiing* and *chess* share one semantic feature, say (Outdoor), and share it in the sense that one is marked + for it and the other −. However, if the hearer of (51) does interpret B's utterance as conveying a contrast between Mary's liking for outdoor activities and Anne's preference for indoor ones, then it is because of her knowledge of the world rather than because of his knowledge of the meaning of the words uttered. We surely do not want the existence of indoor skiing and outdoor chess games to be a logical impossibility. Moreover, it is not clear from the linguistic properties of this utterance that this is the contrast the hearer is expected to recover. The speaker might have been trying to convey a contrast between Mary's non-intellectual personality and Anne's intellectual personality, or between Mary's fitness and Anne's lack of it, etc.

In fact, it is possible that the speaker may not have had any particular contrast in mind. Speakers do not always have specific expectations as to the way their utterances will be interpreted. In many cases the hearer is free to recover any of a range of contextual effects. The main point, however, is that in a case like (52) it is likely that the main relevance of the utterance does not lie just in the identification of the activities that Mary and Anne like, but more in the fact that these activities are different. That is, the hearer is expected to recover two parallel sets of contextual implications each member of which predicates a property incompatible with the property in the corresponding implication in the other set. Thus for example, the relevance of (52) may be understood to lie in the fact that it licenses the derivation of any of the pairs of implications in (54):

(54) Mary is fit.　　　　　　　　Anne is not fit.
　　　Mary likes outdoor　　　　Anne likes indoor activities.
　　　activities.
　　　Mary likes non-intellectual　Anne likes intellectual
　　　pursuits.　　　　　　　　　pursuits.

Obviously, the same point applies to all the examples just given.

Now, there are linguistic clues the speaker may use to indicate that the hearer is expected to process her utterance in a context that enables her to derive such pairs of implications. Most notably, perhaps, we have the parallel intonation patterns illustrated in (55):

(55)(a)　Susan is ˇtall. Mary is ˋshort.
　　(b)　Mary likes ˇskiing. Anne plays ˋchess.

It will be recognized that the use of so-called contrast *but* is often associated with this sort of intonation pattern. The question is whether *but* is used, along with the intonation, simply to constrain the hearer's choice of context so that she can recover two sets of contrasting implications.

If *but* did play this role, then we could reconcile it with the use exemplified in (36) and (40) by saying that *but* instructs the hearer to process the utterance containing it in a context that enables her to establish an incompatibility. In the extreme case (the denial case) the incompatibility is between propositions – it is a logical inconsistency – with the result that the hearer abandons one in favour of the other. In the contrast case the incompatibility is simply between predicates, and the hearer is simply expected to interpret each of the propositions presented as predicating a property (or set of properties) which cannot be true of anything with the property (or set of properties) understood to be predicated by the other. In other words, she is simply expected to interpret each proposition in, for example, (47) as drawing attention to the respect or the respects in which Susan and Mary are different from each other.

However, this is not the whole story. If *but* were used simply in the way I have just outlined, then it ought to be possible to use it in any utterance where the speaker is understood to be drawing attention to the difference between two things, and there are at least two such cases where the use of *but* is impossible. Notice first that so far all our examples of contrast have involved only one speaker. However, it is possible for the second speaker of a dialogue to produce an utterance that is understood to convey a contrast with the state of affairs described by the first. Suppose you and I have just met and we are telling each other about our backgrounds. As is usual in such conversations, we discover some similarities – you like jazz, so do I, etc. – and some differences – your parents vote Labour, mine Tory. Whereas in this situation it would be quite appropriate for me to respond to your utterance in (56) with the one in (57)(a), the one in (57)(b) would be odd:

(56)   You: My parents vote Labour.
(57)(a) Me: Mine vote Tory.
   (b) Me: But mine vote Tory.

The problem is not that *but* cannot be used to introduce a new utterance. There are situations in which the utterance of (57)(b) would be perfectly acceptable. The problem is that all these are situations in which I would be understood to be denying an assumption derived from your utterance, a fact which might be taken to suggest that my example simply provides further evidence for the dichotomy between the two *but*s. However, if there is a contrast *but*, then it is difficult to see why (57)(b) cannot be understood in the same way as (57)(a).

The second problem becomes evident once it is recognized that our examples of contrast are restricted to cases in which the speaker is drawing attention to the difference, or differences, between just two things. It is also possible for a speaker to draw attention to the respects in which several things are different from each other. Consider, for example, (58) and (59):

(58) Susan is tall, Mary is short, and Anne is of average height.
(59) Mary votes Labour, Susan votes SDP, Anne votes Tory, and Jane votes for the Communist Party.

The fact that *but* cannot be used in such cases is related to the well-known (but as far as I know unexplained) observation that whereas *and* can conjoin any number of propositions, *but* can only be used to connect two, an observation which is difficult to reconcile with the claim that *but* (in its contrast use) has 'and' as part of its meaning.

Notice that in this case it doesn't much matter in which order the conjuncts are presented. Reverse any of the conjuncts of (59) and you still recover the interpretation in which Mary, Susan, Anne, and Jane are all different from each other in respect of who they vote for. However, it is possible to have what appears to be a conjunction in which one conjunct is understood to be relevant by virtue of suggesting a contrast with the rest. For instance, we might interpret the final conjunct of (60) as being relevant in virtue of contrasting with all the others. In this case the order of conjuncts does matter. This interpretation is not possible for (61):

(60) Mary votes Labour, Susan SDP, Anne Tory, and Jane doesn't bother.
(61) Mary votes Labour, Susan SDP, Jane doesn't bother, and Anne votes Tory.

It is in this kind of case that we might substitute *but*. That is, it seems that (62) is a more explicit way of conveying the suggestion we recovered from (60). Notice that the *but*-'conjunct' cannot go just anywhere. The only interpretation possible for (63) is one in which the final two conjuncts form a conjunction (a unit) that is relevant by virtue of conveying a contrast between Jane and Anne on the one hand and Mary and Susan on the other:

(62) Mary voted Labour, Susan SDP, Anne Tory, but Jane didn't bother.
(63) Mary voted Labour, Susan SDP, but Jane didn't bother and Anne voted Tory.

What this seems to suggest is that when *but* means contrast it can only be used to draw attention to a binary opposition. However, if *but* can be used to draw attention to the fact that two things are different from each other, why can't it be used to indicate that several things are different from each other? Notice, too, that *but* isn't just used to indicate that there is a difference between Jane on the one hand and Mary, Susan, and Anne on the other, for then (62) would be equivalent to (64), which, it seems, it isn't:

(64) Jane didn't bother voting, but Mary voted Labour, Susan SDP, and Anne voted Tory.

Let us look at (59) and (62) more closely. One of the differences between these two examples is that whereas the former is interpreted in a context in which Mary, Susan, Anne, and Jane all voted for someone, the latter is not. Indeed, the whole point of (62) seems to lie in the fact that Jane didn't vote. As I have already suggested, the point of (59) may be regarded as lying not simply in the identification of who each person voted for, but more in the fact that who they voted for is different. That is, the hearer may derive four parallel sets of contrasting implications. But notice that these implications are derived in the same context. That is, there is a sense in which the hearer establishes the relevance of the whole conjunction in the same context, or in other words, in which each conjunct is relevant only by virtue of being part of a conjunction that is consistent with the Principle of Relevance. It is no more relevant to know, for example, that Mary did not vote SDP than it is to know that Susan did not vote Labour, and so on. Hence the possibility of reversing the order of the conjuncts without any change of interpretation.

I have suggested that, intuitively speaking, the whole point of (62) seems to lie in the fact that Jane didn't vote. Actually this isn't quite the whole story. Saying that Jane didn't vote in the context of the rest of the utterance in (62) is not the same as saying it in the context of (65) or (66):

(65) Is there anyone who didn't vote?
(66) A $20 fine will be imposed on anyone who didn't vote.

Notice that the suggestion is that the first part of the utterance serves as the context for the interpretation of the *but*-proposition.

If this is right, and *but* indicates how the proposition it introduces is relevant, given this context, then we haven't got a conjoined proposition that is consistent with the Principle of Relevance, but rather a *discourse connection* of the kind mentioned earlier. It would also explain the asymmetry between (62) and (64). And given that there is this asymmetry, it explains why *but* cannot be used to connect more than two propositions.

Let me finish by outlining briefly how the constraint *but* imposes in these contrast sorts of cases is related to the one it imposes in the denial sort of cases. Why would it be relevant to know that Jane doesn't vote, given that Susan, Mary, and Anne do? There seem to be two sorts of answer. First, it might be relevant to know that Jane doesn't vote because the information in the first part of the utterance gave rise to the assumption that Jane does vote: if Susan, Mary and Anne do, then Jane must. In this case the *but*-clause will be interpreted in exactly the same way as the *but*-clauses in (37) and (41) – that is, as a denial of an expectation. Notice that in this case the connection cannot be left implicit in the way it is left implicit in (60). The hearer has to be told that she was expected to have derived the assumption that Jane voted from the first part of the utterance.

I shall have to give the second sort of answer in a more round-about way. Suppose that the hearer had access to the assumption in (67)(a):

(67)(a) If Jane is like Mary, Susan, and Anne, then she would have voted.

In this context the proposition that Jane did not vote would be relevant by virtue of the fact that it enables the deduction of the conclusion in (67)(b):

(67)(b) Jane is not like Susan, Mary, and Anne.

There are all sorts of reasons why the speaker might believe that it is relevant to establish the truth of (67)(b) – among them her belief that the hearer assumed that Jane was like Susan, Mary, and Anne. Obviously, if Jane is not like Susan, Mary, and Anne then Susan, Mary, and Anne are not like Jane. However, when we look at how this conclusion was derived it seems that this symmetry is only apparent. As I have described it, the deduction of this conclusion hinges on the proposition that Jane did not vote – that is, the proposition in the *but*-clause – and not the proposition that the others did vote. That is, the relevance of the proposition introduced by *but* lies in the fact that it constitutes a denial of the consequent of the conditional premise in (67)(a). In contrast, in (64) it is the proposition that Mary and the others voted that is relevant as a denial, and the hearer will be expected to derive the conclusion that Mary and the others are not like Jane. I give the inference in (68):

(68)(a) If Mary etc. were like Jane, then they would not have voted.
 (b) They did vote. (Premise in *but*-clause)
 (c) Mary etc. are not like Jane. (Conclusion)

I do not wish to suggest that the first clause plays no role at all in the interpretation of these utterances. Let us return to (62), and consider why the hearer might be considered to have access to the conditional premise in (67)(a). Notice that whereas in (59) the relevance of the utterance lay in the identity of the parties each person voted for, in (62) the identity of those parties no longer seems important. What is important is the fact that Susan, Mary, and Anne voted (for someone). The suggestion is that the hearer is expected to recognize that the relevance of the first clause lies in the identification of a property the possession of which is incompatible with the property understood to have been attributed to Jane, or in other words, in the identification of the property the speaker considers relevant to a proof or disproof of Jane's similarity with Susan, Mary, and Anne. To draw attention to a contrast, after all, is to draw attention to the respect in which two things are not similar.

However, as we have seen, the speaker of (62) is not just drawing attention to the respect in which two sets of things are different from each other. The contrast gives the hearer access to a conditional proposition – the antecedent specifying the poles and the consequent the respect in which they are understood to contrast – whose consequent is denied by the proposition introduced by *but*. It is this relationship between contrast and denial that provides a key to the relationship between the so-called denial and contrast uses of *but*.

My aim in this section has been to show that all uses of *but* can be analysed in terms of a single constraint on relevance. Since this constraint is a constraint on the relevance of the proposition it introduces, then by the arguments of section 4.3, *but* cannot be said to have 'and' as part of its meaning. It cannot be said to form a conjunction consistent with the Principle of Relevance. Rather it indicates how the relevance of the proposition it introduces is dependent on the interpretation of another. This suggests that the fact that a sentence is syntactically co-ordinate does not necessarily mean that it will be used to express a conjoined proposition. That is, it suggests that there may be a discrepancy between syntactic representation and propositional form.

This conclusion will certainly be unpalatable to those who still (after the arguments presented earlier in this book) believe that there is no gap between syntactic representation and propositional form, or, in other words, that the proposition expressed by an utterance is fully determined by its linguistic properties. On the other hand, given the role of the context and the Principle of Relevance in the identification of propositional content, the fact that the syntactic form of the sentence uttered does not correspond to the form of the proposition recovered should not be surprising.

But surely, it may be objected, there is a difference between being indeterminate or underspecified and being misleading. It is one thing to give the hearer an incomplete clue as to the proposition she is expected to recover and quite another to give her a misleading one. Perhaps this is right. However, it is worth pointing out that this is not the only example of such a discrepancy. Syntactically speaking, *because* is a subordinating conjunction. However, as we have seen, an utterance like (69) can be interpreted either as stating the cause of his departure or as providing evidence for the belief that he has left:

(69) He has left because his wife's not here.

In the latter interpretation *because* is expressing what I have described as a relation of dependent relevance. That is, it indicates how the proposition it introduces is relevant with respect to the first proposition. Obviously, the speaker may make her intentions explicit by the introduction of a tone-group boundary between the two clauses. However, tone-group boundaries are notoriously unreliable indicators of propositional structure. Moreover, there are examples of discrepancies between linguistic form and propositional interpretation which do not involve co-ordination or subordination. Thus, for example, from a linguistic point of view *it* is referential. However, when *it* is used as the subject of a 'weather verb', as in (70), no reference will be understood to have been made:

(70) It is raining.

The discrepancy I have argued for in this section seems more serious, however. As many readers will have observed, *but* may be embedded in the scope of *if . . . then*. Consider, for example, the conditional in (71):

(71) If Susan is coming but Jane is not, then I shall cancel the lecture.

Notice that as it is used here *but* could not be construed in its so-called 'denial' sense. The objection, if it is valid at all, is an objection only to my analysis of 'contrast' *but*. Notice too that the contrastive suggestion conveyed by *but* does not itself contribute to the truth conditions of (71). The suggestion is simply that the antecedent of (71) must be a conjoined proposition and hence that *but* (in its contrast use) does in fact have 'and' as part of its meaning.

At this point we might simply accept that *but* is ambiguous between an entirely non-truth-conditional (denial) sense in which it imposes a constraint on the relevance of the proposition it introduces and a partly non-truth-conditional (contrast) sense in which it imposes a constraint on the relevance of the conjoined proposition it forms. While this strategy may be in keeping with the main thesis of this book it is not in keeping with its Gricean spirit. Nor can it be reconciled with the facts described earlier in this section. However, it is not clear that it is necessary. For the utterance in (71) is a counter-example to my unified non-truth-conditional analysis of *but*, only given the assumption that sets of assumptions cannot fall under the scope of logical operators. As Deirdre Wilson (personal communication) has pointed out, there are examples suggesting that this assumption cannot be maintained. For instance, the antecedent of (72) is not a conjoined proposition and yet each component proposition falls under the scope of the conditional:

(72) If you want to leave, you really really want to leave, then I'll let you.

The same point applies to the utterance in (73):

(73) If you do this: turn left at the church, then you'll get there in five minutes.

In view of such examples and the gap between linguistic form and propositional content, there is no reason to think that the antecedent of the conditional in (71) is a conjunction and that a unified entirely non-truth-conditional analysis of *but* is not possible.

4.6 Concluding Remarks

In chapter 1 I argued that a semantic representation – the output of the grammar – is not a proposition, but a *logical form* or *blueprint* for a proposition, and it is the task of pragmatic theory to explain how this blueprint is turned into a complete proposition which is integrated into the hearer's existing representation of the world. However, I also warned that there was more to linguistic meaning than this – that there were linguistically specified devices whose contribution to the interpretation of the utterances that contain them cannot be defined in terms of a contribution to propositional content, but must be analysed in terms of constraints on the relevance of the proposition that has taken to be expressed.

I have attempted to demonstrate this aspect of linguistic meaning by examining the role of a limited range of English expressions. As I have emphasized throughout, these expressions impose constraints on relevance in virtue of the inferential connections they express. While their analysis has allowed me to underline the inferential nature of the processes involved in the assessment of relevance, my particular choice of examples may have suggested a misleadingly narrow conception of a semantic constraint on relevance. For not all expressions that impose constraints on relevance express inferential connections. Thus, for example, the use of *anyway* in (74) indicates that the proposition it introduces is relevant in a context that does not include the immediately preceding remark.

(74) Last weekend we went to Winchester with Simon and Jane. They've got a Ford now. Anyway, when we got there we found that the Cathedral was closed.

It is hoped that although I have not by any means given an exhaustive account of either the inferential connectives in English or the range of non-truth-conditional phenomena in English, my treatment of this small range of expressions within the framework of Relevance Theory may provide the basis for future work in these areas in English and in other languages.

This work need not be work on the analysis of the meanings of lexical items, but it may extend to the analysis of the role of certain syntactic constructions and of prosodic devices. That intonation interacts with the meanings of lexical items to constrain pragmatic interpretation should be apparent from my analyses of *also* and *but*. However, the reader will have noticed that the use of each of the inferential connectives I have considered is often associated with a characteristic intonation pattern. Indeed, in some cases the expression may be replaced by intonation for the same effect. Thus, for example, the effect of the use of *after all* in (75) may be gained by the intonation pattern given in (76):

(75) You will have to invite him. After all, he's your brother.
(76) You will have to invite him. He /is your/ ˇbrother.

(Here / denotes a foot boundary so that it is accented, and ˇdenotes a fall–rise.)

Moreover, it seems that intonation may be associated with the distinction I have drawn between connections within the content of utterances and discourse connections. As I remarked in chapter 3, the expressions that make the latter types of connection explicit – that is, the inferential connectives – are typically 'comma-ed off' from the rest of the utterance. That is, they are parenthetical. This means that they provide an intonational break between the two clauses they connect. It would be interesting to compare their role in interpretation with other parentheticals – for example, with appositive relative clauses – and to examine the notion of a tone group – which has been notoriously resistant to definition in purely phonological terms – from the point of view of pragmatic interpretation, and, in particular, from the point of view of the account of discourse connections outlined in this study.

While all this work must be grounded in a psychologically adequate theory of the role of non-linguistic information in utterance interpretation, it will nevertheless be work on the grammatical properties of utterances. That is, it will be part of the study of linguistic semantics. However, it will not be part of linguistic semantics as it was defined in chapter 1 above. For, according to that definition, a semantic representation is a logical form – that is, a representation developed into a complete proposition on the basis of the context and the Principle of Relevance. The constituents of this representation have meanings in the sense that they are mapped onto concepts – addresses for certain logical, lexical, and encyclopedic information. As we have seen, a concept may contain only a logical entry. That is, it will contain only computational information. For example, the concept represented by *and* will include the rule in (77):

(77) and–elimination
    Input: P & O
    Output: (a) P
               (b) Q

Notice that although this is purely computational information it requires the existence of representational information. In particular, it applies to a propositional representation of which *and* is a part.

Now, it could be said that the meanings of expressions like *after all* and *you see* must be analysed in purely computational terms. Each instructs the hearer to perform certain (inferential) computations. However, I have shown that the computations that the hearer performs in accordance with those instructions are not performed over representations that include the meaning of *after all* or *you see*. Neither of these expressions contributes to the truth conditions of the utterances that contain them. In other words, these expressions do not map onto concepts that are constituents of proposition – except, of course, in the (relatively uninteresting) metatheoretical cases in which, for example, one might produce (78) as a description of one's own understanding of the role of *after all*:

(78) A proposition introduced by *after all* must be interpreted as a premise.

In the same way, while one can undoubtedly make metatheoretic statements about the phenomenon of focus it is not the case that the cleft construction in (79) or the heavy stress in (80) represent concepts. They simply instruct the hearer to access a particular kind of context.

(79) It was Tom who drank the beer.
(80) TOM drank the beer.

If *after all* and *you see* do not represent concepts, then by the definition given earlier they cannot be part of the level of semantic representation called 'logical form'. This suggests a non-unitary theory of linguistic semantics. On the one hand, there is the essentially *conceptual* theory that deals with the way in which elements of linguistic structure map onto concepts – that is, onto constituents of propositional representations that undergo computations. On the other, there is the essentially *procedural* theory that deals with the way in which elements of linguistic structure map directly onto computations themselves – that is, onto mental processes. I do not wish to suggest that the former is well understood. However, I hope that in this book I have been able to demonstrate that a complete account of the relationship between linguistic form and pragmatic interpretation must include not just a theory of logical form, but also a theory of grammatically specified constraints on pragmatic computation.

Notes

1 The Domain of Pragmatics

1. Gazdar's approach is adopted by a number of other writers – e.g. Karttunen (1974) and Stalnaker (1972). I cite Gazdar here because his is a particularly clear statement of the position.
2. For an introduction to Montague semantics see Dowty et al. (1981).
3. For a critical assessment of speech act theory see Sperber and Wilson (1986), ch. 4.
4. The suggestion in (6) may be recognized as a quantity implicature. For further discussion of this notion see Gazdar (1979), Horn (1972), and Levinson (1983). Carston (1985) has argued that these suggestions should not be analysed as implicatures, but as pragmatically determined aspects of propositional content.
5. Gettier (1963) has isolated a number of difficulties with the classical definition of knowledge. See also Ayer (1956).
6. Kempson (1986a, 1986b) has argued that the interpretation of anaphoric expressions shows not only that the grammar delivers (incomplete) logical forms which are interpreted as complete propositions on the basis of the context, together with the pragmatic principles, but also that the principles of grammar constrain the process of proposition construction in that the identification of an antecedent value for an anaphoric expression is subject to the binding principles (cf. Chomsky 1981).
7. The Manner Maxim has an overall instruction. 'Be perspicuous.' The Gricean explanation for the interpretation of conjoined utterances hinges on the sub-maxim 'Be orderly.'
8. See 4.2.
9. Grice did not use the term *semantic* either. However, it seems clear that he intended the term *what is said* to refer to the conventional

(i.e. linguistically specified) meaning of an utterance. Since he accepted that such meaning can contribute to what is implicated (or, in other words, that there are conventional implicatures), it seems that he could not have intended the notion of what is said to be coextensive with truth-conditional content. For further discussion see 3.1.

10 A notable exception here is Katz (1972) who points out that since the reference of referring expressions can depend on the assumption that the maxims are being obeyed, "determining what is said depends on the principles for working out what is implicated" (1972: 449).

11 This definition is based on the one given by Schiffer (1972).

2 Relevance and Communication

1 As we shall see in ch. 4, these suggestions should not be analysed as implicatures, but as pragmatically determined elements of what is said. However, the point being made here is that, because they depend on the context, it is always possible for the sentence to be uttered in a context in which they cannot be recovered.

2 See Gazdar 1979: 55–9 for details.

3 All the arguments in this section are due to Sperber and Wilson (1986).

4 The fact that propositions are psychological representations means that they are objects of various propositional attitudes – for example, belief, where the proposition is entertained as a factual description of a state of affairs, or desire, where the proposition is a description of a desirable state of affairs. The concerns of this study are mainly restricted to the interpretation of utterances that express a factual attitude. However, as Sperber and Wilson (1986) show, the framework described in this chapter can be applied to utterances that express non-factual attitudes.

5 See Sperber and Wilson 1986: 108–10 for a more detailed argument for this generalization.

6 See Pulman (1983) and Carston (in preparation) for further discussion of these issues.

7 See Sperber and Wilson 1986: 112–14 for a detailed argument for this point.

8 See Pulman (1983) and Carston (in preparation) for discussion of these questions.

9 cf. Quine (1964).

Notes

10 For an account of these notions see Brown and Yule (1983), and Rumelhart and Norman (1985). For a critical evaluation of the role that these notions play in utterance comprehension see Dresher and Hornstein (1976).
11 See 4.1 for further discussion of this difference.

3 Linguistic Form and Pragmatic Interpretation.

1 Gazdar(1979) criticizes Karttunen's analysis of *manage, fail*, and *try* on the grounds that the suggestions they convey are not conventional implicatures, but generalized conversational implicatures. However, Gazdar's objection does not apply to Grice's original examples of conventional implicature or, indeed, to any of the cases of non-truth-conditional linguistic meaning discussed in the following sections.
2 Karttunen (1971) calls these implicative verbs.
3 Notice that the *because*-clause may be intonationally separated and still express a causal relationship between states of affairs.
4 Notice that Kempson herself uses *therefore* (1975: 215) in a way that cannot be understood in terms of the causal analysis she advocates.
5 For an account of the role of inference in the interpretation of utterances conveying non-factual attitudes see Sperber and Wilson (1986).
6 For further discussion of this notion see Sperber and Wilson 1986: 143-4.
7 To some extent the distinction I am drawing here between inferential and causal connections corresponds to Halliday and Hasan's (1976) distinction between internal and external cohesive ties. However, they consider *so* to be ambiguous between an internal (inferential) sense and an external (causal) sense.
8 For interesting work along these lines see Gutt (1985) and Blass (in preparation).
9 See 4.5 for discussion of these connotations.
10 See also Reinhart (1982).
11 This means that an utterance containing *also* must be preceded by an utterance that supplies not just a value for the variable substituted for the focused constituent, but a value distinct from the one focus is being used to draw attention to. I have captured this above by saying that an utterance like (70) must be preceded by an utterance that supplies a value for the variable *did something else*. But notice that the *else* does not have to be written into the meaning of

also since it follows from the Principle of Relevance, together with the fact that the background of an utterance containing *also* is a conjunction.

4 Relevance and Coherence: Discourse Connectives

1. The term *coherence* is standardly used to describe 'semantic' continuity or connectivity of content, and is contrasted with *cohesion* which is textual unity created by cohesive (i.e. linguistic) devices (cf. Halliday and Hasan 1976). My concern with the contribution of linguistic form to pragmatic interpretation might seem to suggest that I should have entitled this chapter 'Relevance and Cohesion'. But my point in this section is that an account of the contribution of linguistic form to the interpretation of discourse is grounded in an account of coherence which itself is grounded in an account of relevance.
2. This point is also made by Brown and Yule (1983).
3. See Posner (1980) for a survey of such examples. Some readers may recognize such suggestions as examples of what H. Clark (1977) has called *bridging implicatures*.
4. It will be recognized that *and* is not always used to form a conjoined proposition consistent with the Principle of Relevance. When stressed, it may be taken to introduce a proposition consistent with the Principle of Relevance, a use often represented orthographically by giving it a capital letter – this is, by making it sentence-initial. It would be interesting to analyse the role of stressed *and* in terms of the framework being developed in this book. Here I shall simply say that in this use *and* is not equivalent to truth-functional co-ordinating *and*.
5. There is an interpretation for this utterance which may appear to be similar to the denial of expectation interpretation in which the speaker is taken to be proving the falsity of the claim that all Republicans are dishonest. However, notice that the success of the proof hinges on the truth of the conjunction. That is, it is the conjunction that is relevant.

References

Austin, J. L. (1962) *How to Do Things with Words*. Oxford: Clarendon Press.
Ayer, A. J. (1956) *The Problem of Knowledge*. London: Penguin.
Bach, K. and Harnish, R. (1979) *Linguistic Communication and Speech Acts*. Cambridge, Mass.: MIT Press.
Blass, R. (1985) 'Cohesion, coherence and relevance'. University College London, unpublished MS.
Boden, M. (1977) *Artificial Intelligence and Natural Man*. Sussex: Harvester Press.
Brown, G. and Yule, G. (1983) *Discourse Analysis*. Cambridge: Cambridge University Press.
Carston, R. (1984) 'Semantic and Pragmatic Analyses of and'. Paper read at the Spring Meeting of the Linguistics Association of Great Britain 1984.
Carston, R. (1985) 'Saying and Implicating'. Paper read at the Cumberland Lodge Conference on Logical Form.
Carston, R. (in preparation) *Word Meaning and Concepts*. University College London Doctoral Dissertation.
Chomsky, N. (1980) *Rules and Representations*. Oxford: Blackwell.
Chomsky, N. (1981) *Lectures on Government and Binding*. Dordrecht: Foris.
Chomsky, N. (1986) *Knowledge of Language: Its Nature, Origin, and Use*. New York: Praeger.
Clark, H. and Marshall, C. (1981) 'Definite reference and mutual knowledge', in A. Joshi, B. Webber, and I. Sag (eds), *Elements of Discourse Understanding*. Cambridge: Cambridge University Press.
Clark, H. (1977) 'Bridging' in P. Johnson-Laird and P. Wason (eds), *Thinking: Readings in Cognitive Science*. Cambridge: Cambridge University Press.

References

Cohen, L. J. (1971) 'Some remarks on Grice's views about the logical particles of natural languages', in Y. Bar-Hillel (ed.), *Pragmatics of Natural Languages*. Dordrecht: Reidel.

Cresswell, M. J. (1973) *Logics and Languages*. London: Methuen.

Dascal, M. and Katriel, T. (1977) 'Between semantics and pragmatics: the two types of "but" – Hebrew "aval" and "ela"', *Theoretical Linguistics* 4: 143–72.

Dowty, D. R., Walls, R., and Peters, S. (1981) *Introduction to Montague Semantics*. Dordrecht: Reidel.

Dresher, B. E. and Hornstein, N. H. (1976) 'On the supposed contribution of artificial intelligence to the scientific study of language', *Cognition* 4: 321–98.

Fodor, J. A. (1976) *The Language of Thought*. Hassocks, Sussex: Harvester Press.

Fodor, J. A. (1981a) *Representations*. Cambridge, Mass.: MIT Press.

Fodor, J. A. (1981b) 'The present status of the innateness controversy'. Reprinted in J. A. Fodor 1981a 251–316.

Fodor, J. A. (1981c) 'Methodological solipsism considered as a research strategy in cognitive psychology'. Reprinted in J. A. Fodor 1981a: 225–53.

Fodor, J. A. (1983a) *The Modularity of Mind*. Cambridge, Mass.: MIT Press.

Fodor, J. A. (1983b) 'Mental representations: an introduction', MIT: unpublished MS.

Fodor, J. A. and Fodor, J. D. (1980) 'Functional structure, quantifiers, and meaning postulates', *Linguistic Inquiry* 11: 759–69.

Fodor, J. A., Garrett, M., Walker, E. and Parkes, C. (1980) 'Against definitions'. *Cognition* 8.3: 263–367.

Gazdar, G. (1979) *Pragmatics: Implicature, Presupposition and Logical Form*. New York: Academic Press.

Gettier, E. L. (1963) 'Is justified true belief knowledge?', Analysis 23. 121–3. Reprinted in A. Phillips Griffiths (ed.) (1967) *Knowledge and Belief*. Oxford: Oxford University Press.

Grice, H. P. (1967) 'Logic and Conversation'. William James Lectures, Harvard University. Unpublished MS.

Grice, H. P. (1975) 'Logic and Conversation', in P. Cole and J. Morgan (eds), *Syntax and Semantics*, Vol. 3 *Speech Acts*. New York: Academic Press. 41–58.

Grice, H. P. (1978) 'Further notes on logic and conversation', in P. Cole (ed.), *Syntax and Semantics*, Vol. 9. *Pragmatics*. New York: Academic Press. 113–28.

Gutt, E. (1985) 'Towards an analysis of pragmatic connectives in Silt'i'. University College London, unpublished MS.

Halliday, M. A. K. and Hassan, R. (1976) *Cohesion in English*. London: Longman.

Hobbs, J. R. (1977) 'Coherence and Interpretation in English Texts' *Proc. IJCAI*. Cambridge, Mass.

Hobbs, J. R. (1978) 'Why is discourse coherent?' Technical Note 176, SRI Projects 5844, 7510, 7910.

Horn, L. R. (1972) 'On the semantic properties of the logical operators in English'. Indiana Linguistic Club Mimeo.

Johnson-Laird, P. N. (1983) *Mental Models*. Cambridge: Cambridge University Press.

Karttunen, L. (1971) 'Implicative verbs', *Language* 47: 340–58.

Karttunen, L. (1974) 'On pragmatic and semantic aspects of meaning', paper presented at the 11th Annual Philosophy Colloquium.

Karttunen, L. and Peters, S. (1975) 'Conventional implicature in Montague Grammar'. Berkeley Linguistics Society 1.

Katz, J. (1972) *Semantic Theory*. New York: Harper and Row.

Kempson, R. M. (1975) *Presupposition and the Delimitation of Semantics*. Cambridge: Cambridge University Press.

Kempson, R. (1986a) 'Logical form: The grammar–cognition interface'. Unpublished MS.

Kempson, R. (1986b) 'Definite NPs and context dependence'. In T. Myers (ed.), *Reasoning and Discourse Processes*. London: Academic Press.

Kripke, S. (1972) 'Naming and Necessity' in D. Davidson and G. Harman (eds), *Semantics of Natural Language*. Dordrecht: Reidel.

Lakoff, G. (1970) 'Some thoughts on transderivational constraints', in B. B. Kachru et al. (eds), *Papers in Honor of Henry and Renee Kahane*. Urbana: University of Illinois Press.

Lakoff, G. (1971) 'Presuppositions and relative well-formedness', in D. D. Steinberg and Jakobovits, L. A. (eds), *Semantics: An Interdisciplinary Reader*. Cambridge: Cambridge University Press.

Lakoff, R. (1971) 'If's, and's and but's about conjunction', in C. J. Fillmore and D. T. Langendoen (eds), *Studies in Linguistic Semantics*. New York: Holt, Reinhart, and Winston.

Levinson, S. (1983) *Pragmatics*. Cambridge: Cambridge University Press.

Lewis, D. (1969) *Convention*. Cambridge, Mass.: Harvard University Press.

Lewis D. (1972) 'General semantics', in D. Davidson and G. Harman (eds), *Semantics of Natural Language*. Dordrecht: Reidel.

Lewis, D. (1979) 'Scorekeeping in a Language Game', in R. Bauerle et al. (eds), *Semantics from Different Points of View*. Berlin: Springer Verlag.

MacLaran, R. (1982) 'The Semantics and Pragmatics of the English Demonstratives'. Cornell University: Unpublished Doctoral Dissertation.

Minsky, M. (1975) 'A Framework for Representing Knowledge', in P. Winston (ed.), *The Psychology of Computer Vision*. New York: McGraw-Hill.

Montague, R. (1972) 'Pragmatics and Intensional Logic', in D. Davidson and G. Harman (eds), *Semantics of Natural Language*. Dordrecht: Reidel.

Posner, R. (1980) 'Semantics and Pragmatics of Sentence Connectives in Natural Language', in J. R. Searle, F. Kiefer, and M. Bierwisch (eds), *Speech Act Theory and Pragmatics*. Dordrecht: Reidel.

Pulman, S. (1983) *Word Meaning and Belief*. London: Croom Helm.

Putnam, H. (1975) 'The meaning of "meaning"'. In H. Putnam, *Mind, Language and Reality: Philosophical Papers* II. Cambridge: Cambridge University Press.

Quine, W. V. O. (1964) 'Two Dogmas of Empiricism' in W. V. O. Quine, *From a Logical Point of View*. Cambridge, Mass.: Harvard University Press.

Reinhart, T. (1982) 'Pragmatics and Linguistics: An Analysis of Sentence Topics'. Distributed by Indiana University Linguistics Club, Bloomington, Ind.

Rumelhart, D. E. and Norman, D. A. (1978) 'Accretion, Tuning and Restructuring: Three Models of Learning', in J. W. Cotton and R. L. Klatzky, (eds), *Semantic Factors in Cognition*. Hillsdale, NJ: Lawrence Erlbaum Ass.

Rumelhart, D. E. and Norman, D. A. (1985) 'Representation of Knowledge', in A. M. Aitkenhead and J. M. Slack (eds), *Issues in Cognitive Modeling*. Hillsdale, NJ: Lawrence Erlbaum Ass.

Samet, J. and Schank, R. (1984) 'Coherence and Connectivity', *Linguistics and Philosophy* 7: 57–82.

Schank, R. and Abelson, R. (1977) *Scripts, Plans, Goals, and Understanding*. Hillsdale, NJ: Lawrence Erlbaum Ass.

Schiffer, S. (1972) *Meaning*. Oxford: Clarendon Press.

Searle, J. A. (1969) *Speech Acts*. Cambridge: Cambridge University Press.

Sperber, D. and Wilson, D. (1981) 'Irony and the Use-Mention Distinction', in P. Cole (ed.), *Radical Pragmatics*. New York: Academic Press.

Sperber, D. and Wilson, D. (1982) 'Mutual Knowledge and Relevance in Theories of Comprehension', in N. Smith (ed.), *Mutual Knowledge*. London: Academic Press.

Sperber, D. and Wilson, D. (1986) *Relevance: Communication and Cognition*. Oxford: Blackwell.

Stalnaker, R. (1972) 'Pragmatics', in D. Davidson and G. Harman (eds), *Semantics of Natural Language*. Dordrecht: Reidel.

Stalnaker, R. (1974) 'Pragmatic Presupposition' in M. Munitz and P. Unger (eds), *Semantics and Philosophy: Studies in Contemporary Philosophy*. New York: New York University Press. 197–213.

Stalnaker, R. (1975) 'Presuppositions', in D. Hockney, W. Harper, and B. Freed (eds), *Contemporary Research in Philosophical Logic and Linguistic Semantics*. Dordrecht: Reidel.

Van Dijk, T. (1977) *Text and Context*. London: Longman.

Wilson, D. (1975) *Presuppositions and Non-Truth-Conditional Semantics*. London: Academic Press.

Wilson, D. and Sperber, D. (1979) 'Ordered Entailments: An Alternative to Presuppositional Theories', in C. K. Oh and D. Dineen (eds), *Syntax and Semantics* 11, *Presuppositions*. New York: Academic Press.

Wilson, D. and Sperber, D. (1981) 'On Grice's Theory of Conversation', in P. Werth (ed.), *Conversation and Discourse*. London: Croom Helm. 155–78.

Wilson, D. and Sperber, D. (1986) 'Inference and Implicature', in C. Travis (ed.), *Meaning and Interpretation*. Oxford: Blackwell.

Index

Abelson, R., 56
accessibility, 10, 14, 20, 32–3, 40, 49, 54, 58, 63, 65–71, 76–7, 81–3, 92, 95, 111; *see also* context; processing effort
accommodation, rule of, 11
addition relation, 97, 98, 103–4; *see also* 'also'; 'moreover'
adverbials of time, 7
'after all', 45, 81–4, 86, 89, 90, 120, 123, 142, 143–4
algorithm, 31; heuristic vs, 37–9
'also', 97–104, 147 n11
ambiguity, 5, 8, 23–4, 62, 78, 80, 115, 125, 140
analytic implications, 47, 48, 49, 82–3
'and', 21–2, 105, 113–21, 125, 130, 143, 148 n4; 'but' vs, 125, 130–1, 135, 139; *see also* conjunction
antonyms, 132
'anyway', 141–2
artificial intelligence, 56
assumptions, 13, 38, 42; abandoning, 52–3, 127–8, 133–4; factual vs non-factual, 80, *see also* factuality; strength of, 42, 51–3, 84, 93–4, 104, 127; *see also* contextual assumptions

Austin, J., 2
Ayer, A.J., 145 n5

Bach, K., 2, 31
'because', 78–9, 81, 139, 147 n3
belief, 16–17; fixation of, 14, 39
Blass, R., 57, 61, 108–10, 147 n8
Boden, M., 113
Brown, G., 107, 147 n10, 148 n2
'but', 125–41; *see also* contrastive interpretation; denial

calculability, of implicatures, 34–9
cancellability, 22, 36, 37–8, 115
Carston, R., 24, 115, 145 n4, 146 n6, 146 n8
causal connection, 78–80, 87–9, 112–15, 117; *see also* 'and'; inferential connection
central system of thought, 13–14, 39
Chomsky, N., 9, 12, 19, 145 n6
chunks of information, 57
Clark, H., 29–30, 117, 148 n3
cleft construction, 74, 99, 144
cognise, 12
cognitive environment, 31–3, 54
Cohen, L.J., 22, 114–15
coherence, 57–8, 105–41, 148 n1;

as derivable from relevance, 111–25
cohesion, 106–7, 148 n1
command, 80–1
common ground, 75; *see also* mutual knowledge; shared knowledge
competence, grammatical, 18–20; performance vs, 18–21; pragmatic, 18–20
computation, 12–13, 17–18, 56, 143–4; *see also* inference rules; inferential connection
concepts, 44, 55–9, 83, 143–4; encyclopedic entry of, 55–9, 83; lexical entry of, 55; logical entry of, 44–5, 55–6, 83
conclusions, 35–7, 41–6, 50–4, 69, 78–91
conditional, 79, 121, 140
confirmation, 14, 39–43, 49–52, 85; *see also* evidence
conjunction, 21–2, 36, 78–80, 95–6, 98–9, 113–24, 131, 135–6, 139; contrast and, 131–41; denial and, 125–31
connectives, logical, *see* logical operators; natural-language, 21–2, 43–4, 79; *see also* 'and'; 'because'; discourse connectives; 'or'
consequence, logical, 73, 78–91; *see also* conclusions, premises
constraints, 18, 20, 40, 75; grammatical, 143–4; *see also* cleft construction; semantic constraints; stress
context, 5–11, 16, 20, 26–33, 48–54, 56–63, 75, 76, 77, 82, 84, 92–5, 105, 108, 109, 110, 111–12, 126, 136; initial, 58, 81–4, 100, 111; *see also* accessibility

context selection, 9–11, 15, 26–33, 39, 58–71; constraints on, 55, 66–71, 75, 76–7, 93, 97, 110–11, 133; *see also* semantic constraints
contextual assumptions, 26–7, 32–3, 38, 55, 56, 62–71, 77, 92, 94, 107, 129
contextual effects, 40, 41, 49, 53–4, 59–71, 77, 86, 101, 111–13, 127–8, 133–4
contextual implications, 48–54, 68, 85–90, 96, 133
contextual prominence, 10–11
contradiction, 3, 41, 52–3, 128
contrastive interpretation, 125, 126, 131–41; *see also* 'but'
contrastive particles, 128; *see also* 'but'
conventional implicature, 4, 35, 72–7; *see also* semantic constraints
conversation, Grice's theory of, 21–7, 34–5, 72–3
conversational implicature, 3, 25–7, 34–9, 63–71, 77, 113–15; bridging, 148 n3; quantity, 38; scalar, 38; strong vs weak, 71, 93; working out schema for, 35
co-ordinates, 8, 10
Cresswell, M., 2

Dascal, M., 125, 129
decomposition, 44
deduction, 35, 38, 39–51, 95–7; *see also* inference rules; logics
definite descriptions, 9–10, 30
definitions, 44
deixis, 6; *see also* indexicals
demonstrative inference, 50; *see also* deduction
demonstratives, 5–8
denial, 125–31, 134, 137–8

deontic modality, 81
disambiguation, 5, 8, 23–4
discourse, 105–11; *see also* coherence
discourse connectives, 105–25, 137; *see also* 'after all'; 'because'; 'moreover'; 'so'; 'therefore'
Dowty, D.R., 145 n2
Dresher, B.E., 147 n10

elaboration relation, 108–9
E-language, 9
elimination rules, 41–5, 47; *although*-elimination, 44; *and*-elimination, 41–2, 55, 143; *bachelor*-elimination, 44; *because*-elimination, 43; conjunctive *modus ponens*, 96; *know*-elimination, 44; *modus ponendo ponens*, 47, 96; *modus tollendo ponens*, 47; *red*-elimination, 45; *sheep*-elimination, 45
ellipsis, 8, 24, 62, 106
encyclopedic information, 55–8; *see also* concepts; context; propositions
enrichment, of logical form, 24–5, 114–19, 121
entailments, 3, 41–3, 45, 99–103; background, 101–3; grammatically specified, 100–3
evidence, 29, 40, 49–53, 78–87, 91–7, 103–4, 120–2; *see also* confirmation
expectation, of relevance, 60; of speaker, 64–70
explanations, 88–90, 118–19, 123, 133; *see also* 'you see'
explicit content, 48, 61, 69–70; *see also* propositional content

factuality, guarantee of, 93–4
focus, 97–104, 144
Fodor, J.A., 13–17, 37, 39, 44, 116
Fodor, J.D., 116
formal operation, 16–17, 41
frames, 56–8, 110
full-stop utterances, 113, 117–19
'furthermore', 91, 97, 119, 120–1

Garrett, M., 44
Gazdar, G., 2–4, 6–7, 15, 18–19, 22, 38, 117–18, 145 n1, 145 n4, 146 n2, 147 n1
Gettier, E.L., 145 n5
grammar, 11–12, 20; text, 57
Grice, H.P., 3, 21–7, 34–7, 69, 70, 71, 72–3, 77, 78, 79, 80, 113, 117, 145 n9, 147 n1
Gricean spirit, 88, 140
Gutt, E., 147 n8

Halliday, M.A.K., 105–8, 147 n7, 148 n1
Harnish, R., 2, 31
Hasan, R., 105–8, 147 n7, 148 n1
Hobbs, J.R., 105–8
Horn, L.R., 145 n4
Hornstein, N.H., 147 n10
hypothesis formation, 14, 39, 40

idealization, 19
I-language, 9
implications, analytic, 47, 48, 49, 82–3; contextual, *see* contextual implications; non-trivial, 47–8; synthetic, 47–8, 50, 82–3; trivial, 46; *see also* deduction; inference rules
implicature, 21–6, 63–71; *see also* conventional implicature; conversational implicature; saying

implicit import, 69–70, 112; *see also* conversational implicature; explicit content
inconsistency, 42, 129–30; *see also* contradiction; denial
indeterminacy, of implicit import, 70–1
index, contextual, 8, 10
indexicals, 5–11, 15
inductive reasoning, 36–9
inference, 13, 16–17, 35–54; *see also* calculability; deduction; inductive reasoning; inferential connection; logics
inference rules, 41–7, 56, 96; *see also* elimination rules; introduction rules
inferential connection, 78–91, 118–19, 122, 141–2; *see also* causal connection
informational encapsulation, 13
information-processing, 12, 40, 54, 56
input system, 13, 39, 48
intention, of speaker, 10, 63–70
intentional property, 16
intonation, 73, 79, 133, 139, 142
introduction rules, 45–6; *and*-introduction, 46, 95–6; double negation, 45; *or*-introduction, 45

Johnson-Laird, P.N., 107
justification, 78–91; *see also* evidence

Karttunen, L., 22, 73–7, 145 n1, 147 n1, 147 n2
Katriel, T., 125, 129
Katz, J., 44, 146 n10
Kempson, R., 2, 18–19, 79–80, 125, 145 n6, 147 n4
knowledge, linguistic vs non-linguistic, 1, 5–6, 11–18, 75, 126, 132; mutual, *see* mutual knowledge; propositional, 12
Kripke, S., 44

Lakoff, G., 126, 129
Lakoff, R., 125–6, 132
language of thought, 15, 116
Levinson, S., 2, 6, 36–8, 50, 145 n4
Lewis, D., 2, 5, 9–11
linguistic form, 4
logical form, 16, 18, 74, 141, 143–4
logical operators, 3, 22, 78–9, 114–15, 140–1; *see also* logical particles
logical particles, 43
logics, 41, 43, 45; classical vs psychologically real, 45–6; completeness of, 43; consistency of, 42; *see also* inference rules

Maclaran, R., 10, 112
Marshall, C., 29–30
maxims of communication, 6, 21–2, 26, 69; maxim of informativeness, 25; maxim of manner, 22, 114, 117–18, 145 n7; maxim of relevance, 24, 25
meaning, 1–2; linguistic, 7, 17; *see also* truth-conditional meaning
meaning postulate, 44–5, 74, 116
memory, 13–14, 30, 41, 55–8
mental models, 107
mental processes, 16, 18, 144; *see also* computation
mental structure, 18–20
mention, vs use of language, 110
methodological solipsism, 16

Minsky, M., 56
modularity, 13, 15
Montague, R., 2, 5, 145 n2
'moreover', 45, 91–7, 98, 104, 119–20, 123
mutual knowledge, 28–31, 64–5, 66, 75; procedure for identifying, 29

natural kind term, 44
negation, 78
non-declaratives, 2
non-demonstrative inference, 50; *see also* inductive reasoning
Norman, D.A., 56, 147 n10

Occam's Razor, 21
opaque context, 17
'or', 21–2

parenthetical, 79, 80, 98, 142
Parkes, C., 44
perception, 13
performance, 19; competence vs, 18–21
Peters, S., 73, 74, 76
Posner, R., 148 n3
possible worlds, 7
pragmatic wastebasket, 2–4
pragmatics, 1, 18–27; semantics vs, 1, 16–18, 74–5, 126
premises, 35–7, 39, 41–4, 50–4, 69, 78–97, 119
presupposition, 73, 99
Principle of Relevance, 54–71, 76, 87, 112, 115–16, 120, 121, 123, 130, 136
probabilistic reasoning, 36–7
procedural semantics, 144
processing effort, 20, 40, 54, 58–63, 65–71, 77, 95, 120, 131
proof, 50, 85–7

propositional attitudes, 12, 146 n4; *see also* belief; knowledge
propositional content, of an utterance, 8, 16, 22–6, 70, 107–8, 112, 114–18, 124, 128, 141; *see also* enrichment; underdetermination
propositions, 13, 15–18, 42, 55–6, 146 n4; *see also* concepts; propositional content
prototype theory, 44
psychological theory, 1, 5, 16, 29–31, 43, 46; logical vs, 50, 67, 96; non-psychological vs, 9–11
Pulman, S., 146 n6, 146 n8
Putnam, H., 44

quantifiers, 3, 5
Quine, W.V.O., 146 n9

reference assignment, 5, 10, 23–4, 62, 112–13
Reinhart, T., 147 n10
relevance, 1, 14, 18, 33, 39–71, 81–4, 85, 86, 89, 90; definition of, 49; dependent, 122–5, 139; guarantee of, 63, 65, 87; maximal, 59–60, 119, 121; optimal, 54, 62–71, 77, 92, 116–17; presumption of, 62–3; *see also* contextual effects; Principle of Relevance; processing effort
reminder, 82
representation, 12–13; conceptual, 12, 13, 15; linguistic, 12; propositional, 13, 15, 30, 41, 56
rules, analytic, 47, 82; linguistic, 12; logical, 41–7; synthetic, 47,

56, 82; truth-preserving, 41–2; see also inference rules
Rumelhart, D.E., 56, 147 n10

salience, 10–11
Samet, J., 57
saying, 21–5; implicating vs, 21, 25, 34; the semantics/pragmatics distinction and, 24, 34
Schank, R., 56, 57
schemas, 56
Schiffer, S., 146 n11
scope, of logical operators, 22, 79, 114–15
scripts, 56–7
Searle, J.A., 2
semantic constraints on relevance, 75–144; see also 'after all'; 'also'; 'because'; 'but'; 'moreover'; 'so'; 'therefore'; 'you see'
semantics, 1, 5–18; formal, 5–11; indexical, 6–11; linguistic, 15, 17, 72–5, 143–4; pragmatics vs, 1, 16–18, 74–5, 126; procedural, 144; see also truth-conditional meaning
sentence-context pairs, 5, 7–11, 57
shared knowledge, 32, 66; see also mutual knowledge
Sissala, 61
'so', 80, 85–90, 106, 119, 121, 123
speech act, theory of, 2
Sperber, D., 14, 23–5, 31, 35, 39–42, 46–7, 48, 52, 54, 55, 56, 57, 58, 59, 60, 61, 68, 69, 70, 71, 72, 93, 96, 100, 101, 115, 116, 122, 123, 126, 145 n3, 146 n3, 146 n5, 146 n7, 147 n5, 147 n6
Stalnaker, R., 2, 73, 75, 145 n1
strengthening, of assumptions, 52, 93–4, 127; see also confirmation; evidence; justification
stress, 79, 101–4; contrastive, 101–4; focal, 79, 101; see also focus
synthetic implications, 47–8, 50, 82–3

temporal relation, 114–17, 121
theory construction, scientific, 14, 39
'therefore', 45, 72–3, 78–84, 87
'too', 73–5
topic, comment vs, 99–100; of discourse, 109–10
truth, 12, 41; analytic, 56; synthetic, 56
truth-conditional content of an utterance, 22, 26, 72
truth-conditional meaning, 2, 8, 12–13, 15–18, 72–5; non-truth-conditional vs, 4, 23, 72–7, 78, 99, 112, 126, 140–1, 143–4; psychological unreality of, 16–17
truth-functional sense, 21, 114, 118; of 'and', 114; non-truth-functional vs, 21

underdetermination of content, 5, 62, 107, 109, 115–17
utterance, 1; interpretation of, 14–15; sentence vs, 5, 11

Van Dijk, T., 57–8, 105, 107, 109–11

Walker, E., 44
Wilson, D., 14, 23–5, 31, 35, 39–42, 46–7, 48, 52, 54, 55, 56, 57, 58, 59, 60, 61, 68, 69, 70, 71, 72, 93, 96, 100, 101, 115, 116, 122, 123, 126, 140, 145 n3, 146 n3, 146 n5, 146 n7, 147 n5, 147 n6

'you see', 88–91, 120, 123, 143–4
Yule, G., 107, 147 n10, 148 n2

Index by Robyn Carston